£5

A HISTORY OF HAMPSHIRE

THE DARWEN COUNTY HISTORY SERIES

A History of Hampshire

BARBARA CARPENTER TURNER

Drawings by Carolyn Lockwood

Cartography by H. S. Parsons

PHILLIMORE

First published 1963
Re-issued 1969, 1976
Second edition 1978

This corrected reprint, 1988, by
PHILLIMORE & CO. LTD.,
Shopwyke Hall, Chichester,
West Sussex, England

ISBN 0 85033 254 0

Printed in Great Britain
at the University Printing House, Oxford

Contents

5

Maps and Plans

List of Illustrations

Acknowledgements

I would like to thank the following for permission to reproduce illustrations: The British Museum (nos. 2 and 12); *Hampshire Chronicle* (nos. 1, 6, 10, 16, 17, 24, 27, 28 and 39); Aerofilms (no. 4); W. R. Carpenter Turner, Esq. (nos. 5 and 22); Winchester City Museum (no. 7); J. L. Jervoise, Esq. (no. 8); R. L. Bowker, Esq. (no. 9); E. A. Sollars, Esq. (no. 11); Hampshire Field Club and Archaeological Society (no. 13); K. Marshall, Esq. (nos. 14, 15a, 15b, 20a and 20b); the late Sir Anthony Tichborne, Bt. (no. 21); C. R. Livermore, Esq. (nos. 25 and 38); D. J. Smith, Esq. (no. 31); Bournemouth Public Library (no. 32); Hampshire County Museum Service (no. 35); *Radio Times*, Hulton Picture Library (no. 42); Donald Insall and Associates (no. 43).

The map of Roman Hampshire on page 18 is reproduced from the Ordnance Survey Map with the sanction of the Controller of H. M. Stationery Office. Crown Copyright reserved. The map of Calleva on page 20 is reproduced by permission of Reading Museum and Art Gallery; the plan of the manor house in Warnford Park on page 37 is reproduced by permission of the Hampshire Field Club and Archaeological Society, and the map of Hampshire re-organised on page 106 by permission of Hampshire County Council.

Preface

The writing of this book would not have been possible if it had not been the author's privilege to have the most generous help from many people. I want to take this opportunity of recording here the debt I owe to the hundreds of people, not all of them academics by any means, but with whom I have had the opportunity of discussing local history in the last 25 years. Some have been patient individuals in lecture groups; others I know only as correspondents; many have been members of our county antiquarian society, the Hampshire Field Club, or of the Historical Association in Hampshire, or of one of the many local societies deeply concerned with local history. I should like to thank them all, especially those who are not professional historians, for their enthusiasm and encouragement; it would be a sad day indeed for Hampshire were the county's history to be of interest only to a handful of qualified technicians.

I want to record also my grateful thanks for the courteous and efficient help given me by the staff of the Hampshire County Record Office ever since it opened in 1947; the help I have had from Curators of Museums at Alton, Portsmouth, Southampton, Reading and Winchester; the help I have had from Public Libraries throughout the county, and in particular from the Borough Librarian at Bournemouth, and from two successive City Librarians at Winchester. Moreover, no historian can live in a vacuum, and I owe more than I can say to those individuals who have so generously shared with me their knowledge of different Hampshire localities or subjects; in particular I am indebted to the Rev. S. E. Hockey, Dr. Alwyn Ruddock, Miss Elsie Sandell, Mr. John Harvey, Mr. F. Emery Wallis, Mr. Victor Bonham-Carter, and Mr. D. G. Watts. I should like to thank the Editor of the *Hampshire Chronicle,* Mrs. Woodhouse, for kindly allowing me to make use of the files of her long-established county newspaper; Mr. G. Gardner, the Bishop's Registrar, and Mr. A. J. Willis, for their help with diocesan records; I want to thank the Dean and Chapter of Winchester Cathedral and their Librarian, the Rev. Canon J. P. Boden, not only for allowing me to consult their archives, but for the privilege of being able to work in the peace of the Cathedral Library. To the Cathedral's Deputy Librarian, Miss Beatrice Forder, I am particularly grateful, and I must record here the debt which all historians of our county—present and future—owe her for the scrupulous care and skill with which she has repaired or is repairing the documents and books of our great county archive collections, at the Winchester City Record Office, at the Hampshire County Office, and in the Cathedral Library. I have been much helped by the skill of my cartographer, Mr. H. S. Parsons, and by the efficiency of Mrs. J. H. Preston who typed my manuscript.

In the making of this book I have been fortunate in my publisher. It has been a great privilege to work with Lord Darwen, and to have the benefit of his widsom and knowledge as a publisher of local history.

BARBARA CARPENTER TURNER
1963

Preface to the Second Edition

I must record my thanks to those who have helped me in differing ways with this, the second edition of *A History of Hampshire*: the Hampshire County Archivist and her staff; the Archivists of the cities of Portsmouth, Southampton and Winchester; the staff of the Portsmouth Local History Library, the Southampton Reference Library, and the Winchester Local History Librarian, Mrs. P. Stevens. I want to thank Miss Elizabeth Lewis of the Winchester City Museum, Mr. Adrian Rance of the Southampton City Museum; Mr. K. J. Barton, Director of the Hampshire County Museum Service, and Mrs. P. M. Pottinger, formerly in charge of the Service's photographic collection; the Hampshire County Council Press and Information Unit; Mr. Peter Gwyn and his successor, Mr. Roger Custance, Archivists to Winchester College. I owe much to useful discussions with active local historians, amongst them Mr. and Mrs. E. Grainger, Mr. N. Baker, Mrs. A. Martineau, Mrs. D. Beresford, Mrs. Wilmot, Mr. C. R. Livermore, and Mr. J. R. Grey. I want to thank my publishers and especially Mr. N. Osborne, for his care and help. I renew my thanks to those mentioned in the first Preface, although some of those friends, in Raleigh's phrase, have been 'surprised by time'. It is good to remember that every generation of local historians builds on the foundations of earlier scholarship, a real reason why the study of local history has proved to be a flourishing craft in the Hampshire of the late 20th century.

BARBARA CARPENTER TURNER
1978

I Hampshire before the Roman Occupation

The first human inhabitants of Hampshire of whom anything is known were brutish hunters, many of whom lived along the river valleys, existing on what they could kill, and making no attempt to farm the land. The climate was damp and cold, and the downs were heavily forested with yew, and difficult of access. The Isle of Wight was part of the mainland, till the waters of the English Channel flowed into the great Solent river system, and cut the Island away, probably destroying much evidence of the life and culture of Mesolithic Hampshire man, of whom it is certain that flint was his essential material. From flint he made his weapons and primitive tools, objects manufactured in enormous quantities on certainly easily-recognised inland sites, at Old Winchester Hill, at Beaulieu, and in the New Forest, some sites near large ponds supplying water-fowl and fish for the makers of flint weapons. At Oakhammer Pond, near Selborne, some 3,000 flint implements were recently recorded. Flint, so long a traditional and local building material in Hampshire was thus the raw material which provided the county's first industry.

In comparison with the people who came after them, these early flint users have left little trace on the Hampshire countryside. Their successors, the peoples of later pre-history, a long period of years before the Roman Conquest at A.D. 43, have left behind much visible and enduring evidence as to their communities, their way of life and particularly their way of burial after death. All over Hampshire can still be seen the great hill forts, the groups of *tumuli*, the barrows of many kinds, the ancient tracks and primitive fields which provide a variety of evidence for the field archaeologist and the excavator.

Later, about 2,000 years before Christ, primitive farmers arrived in Hampshire, who knew how to hoe the land and to domesticate and graze animals. They could make primitive pottery, and wore garments of cowhide, for they could not weave. Some, perhaps were cannibals. The clearance of the chalk downs began. In the districts bordering on Hampshire these Neolithic people built causeway camps (for example, on Windmill Hill, Wiltshire, and on The Trundle, Sussex), where an autumn poleaxing of cattle took place. They buried their dead carefully in communal long barrows like those at Danebury, Moody's Down, Chilbolton Down, and Bevis's Grave (now destroyed) at Portsdown.

In about 1800 B.C., a new invader came to southern England. These Beaker folk, so-called because of the shape of their pottery, buried their dead individually in round barrows. Unlike their predecessors they grew little wheat; their main crop was barley. They still used flints, but had some objects of metal. A girl buried at the top of Stockbridge Down had a small bronze awl in her grave, as well as a beaker. The gradual disappearance of the Beaker folk, or their integration with other cultures marks the beginning of the Bronze Age, when metal objects came into general use.

Bronze was the metal of the rich and various objects which tell so much about these new invaders, their wide trading contacts with the Continent, their warrior aristocracy. Their chief port appears to have been at Hengistbury Head; here have been found ornaments of bronze and amber which may imply trade with the eastern Mediterranean. In the Middle Bronze Age cremation became the usual form of burial; in this and in the Early Bronze period individuals were buried in round barrows of various types of which many can still be seen on or near the ancient ridgeways across the Downs. The Seven Barrows of Burghclere are unusually placed, in a valley, the great group of Popham Beacons form a delightful part of a high downland landscape. There are others on Butser and in the Isle of Wight, where the ancient ridgeway from the Needles has at least 12 barrows scattered on it. Barrows are of distinctive types, bell, disc, saucer, and pond; the great bell-barrow at Bishop's Waltham was probably the burial place of some Bronze Age chieftain.

In about 1000 B.C. new invaders came to Hampshire, Deverel-Rimbury people, called after two of their burial places in Dorset. They left behind many scattered burials in Hampshire, particularly in the Christchurch region, and one of their farms has been excavated at Thorny Down near Boscombe Down East. They herded their cattle in large ranches and enclosures. Two bronze twisted torques found at Plaitford and many other finds on the borders of Hampshire show that they were not just peasant farmers, but wealthy men able to buy goods of quality and of distant origin. A trader's hoard of axes, found at Nether Wallop, are of a type originating in Brittany. It was indeed from north-western France that the next wave of invaders came to Hampshire, urged there perhaps by a need of land and by tribal unrest. Again, their landing-place in the county may have been Hengistbury Head. They were Celtic-speaking users of tools and weapons of iron, practising new and improved methods of farming. Unlike their predecessors, they were practically self-sufficient and widespread trade was not a feature of their economy. They grew large quantities of barley, storing the grain in carefully prepared pits and granaries.

14

As yet nothing is really known of their farm buildings in Hampshire, but these Iron Age farmers, whom archaeologists divide into three successive chronological groups, Iron Age A, B and C, have left some really notable marks on the countryside, for they were the makers of the great hill forts, constructed and reconstructed at different times but intended as places of refuge and defence against further invasion threats from the Continent. Amongst the defences thus constructed in about 250 B.C. are the simple hill forts of Quarley and Ladle Hill, the latter particularly interesting because the wave of invasion apparently died away and the fortification was unfinished. Julius Caesar's defeat of the Venetii of Brittany nearly 200 years later meant that many refugees came to Hampshire and Dorset, some of them landing at Hengistbury Head. The year 56 B.C., therefore, has been called a turning-point in the fortunes of Wessex, and many of these people, whose characteristic weapon was the sling, eventually found refuge in the great fortress of Maiden Castle. Thousands of sling stones were recently found in the defence there, for Maiden became the great tribal headquarters of the refugee Gauls who became known in Wessex as Durotriges, controlling not only Dorset but also the western borders of Hampshire. Some of their primitive coins were minted at Hengist-bury, and it has been suggested, on coin evidence, that their boundary on the east was the Hampshire Avon.

The greater part of Hampshire, however, was eventually possessed by refugees from Caesar's government in Northern Gaul, and though the native inhabitants appear to have tried to secure the county by the re-fortification of some hill forts, notably those along the Test valley at Danebury and Bury Hill, it was an effort made in vain.

In the south-east of the county, the refugee leaders of the Gaulish Atrebates, King Commius, whose first settlement was probably at Selsey, penetrated into Hampshire, and may or may not have been about to get as far north as Silchester before he died in 20 B.C. His son or grandson, Eppillus, was the first British ruler to use the word Rex on his coins. Silchester, known to the Romans as *Calleva Atrebatum*, seems to have been the capital of the Atrebates in Hampshire, but most of their land was eventually conquered by the Catuvellauni of King Cunobelinus (Cymbeline) whose capital was Colchester (*Camulodunum*), and whose son, Caractacus, was too powerful an influence to be left undisturbed by the Roman Emperor Claudius. The civilisation which the Romans found in Hampshire can conveniently be called Celtic, but it was a combination of various elements, and there was no uniform pattern. In the greater part of the county, the dominating influence was that of the later refugee tribes, the Atrebatic and Catuvellaunian peoples whose culture is so often

15

called Belgic, but who controlled many peasants and simple farmers of older non-Belgic Iron Age stock. Political power was in the hands of the warriors and the Druid priests. It would be a mistake to suggest that the Belgae in Hampshire had a culture which surpassed that of their Roman conquerors, but Celtic civilisation did in fact reach a high standard. Belgic invaders brought with them a new type of plough with which they were able to cultivate difficult and heavy land not previously used for grain production. They were thus able to grow vast quantities of cereals which they stored in pits and in large jars; traces of Celtic fields, small and square, survive in many parts of the county. Though recent excavation has revealed little evidence as to the nature of possible Belgic 'towns' in Hampshire, it seems reasonably certain that the hill forts used and re-used by earlier people as places of refuge were not their centres. *Venta Belgarum* may have been one of their marketing towns, as its later Roman name certainly would suggest, but it was not important enough to have a mint. The primitive coinage of Celtic Wessex, a coinage of silver and gold, implies not only trade, and wealthy sections of the community able to purchase luxury goods, but also a desire to imitate that Roman civilisation which was soon to impose its uniformity all over England.

Iron Age farmstead reconstructed: Queen
zabeth II Park, Butser.

King Edgar and his New Minster charter.
S British Museum, Vespasian A VIII (2b))

3. Breamore Church: Anglo-Saxon inscription.

4. Netley Abbey from the air.

5. Core of south-western Norman Tower, Winchester Cathedral.

6. The Manor Farm, Broughton.

7. Prisoners' writings: West Gate, Winchester.

8. Alicia Cowdreye, Nun of Wherwell and sister of Peter Cowdreye of Herriard.

II Roman Hampshire

The real conquest of Britain began in A.D. 43 on the order of the Emperor Claudius. One of the reasons for his decision was the appeal of the last of the Atrebate princes of Hampshire, Verica, against Caractacus, and the violence of 'Cymbeline's' other successors. Southern England could have become a dangerous centre of resistance to Roman rule, and at this point Claudius ordered the conquest of Britain, for she was too independent and her wealth made her a desirable addition to the Roman Empire. The military subjection of Hampshire was part of the successful campaign of the Roman general, Vespasian (the later Emperor) in command of the Second Legion. The capture of Maiden Castle, near Dorchester, was a climax in his campaign, and perhaps implies the subjection of Hampshire. It was certainly accompanied or followed by the annexation of the Isle of Wight. There is no evidence to suggest that the native inhabitants either in the mainland or on the island offered much resistance. Caractacus was betrayed to the Romans by the queen of a rival tribe.

Romano-British girl's head from Otterbourne

Unlike great areas in the north of Britain, the Roman occupation of Hampshire was not primarily of a military nature. Roman local government areas or cantons only partially coincided with the old Celtic tribal boundaries. The power of the Atrebates was not revived, and only a small section of the north of the county was included in their canton. This included the capital *Calleva Atrebatum*, but the Roman town there did not coincide entirely with the older settlement of Silchester. The rest of the coast, including apparently the Isle of Wight, formed a large part of the canton of the Belgae. This canton stretched far to the west, where its chief town was *Aquae Sulis* (Bath), but the eastern, Hampshire sector, included the cantonal capital *Venta Belgarum* (Winchester). In this sector were a number of other important Roman settlements, a port of *Clausentum* (Bitterne, near Southampton) and road stations at *Vindomis* (perhaps on a site at Cuckoo's Corner in Holybourne), and *Brige,* thought perhaps to be the small market town of Stockbridge. The canton of the Belgae, a large area, appears to have been an artificial creation of the Romans who also left some important tribal centres to decline, for example Hengistbury Head, where there had been a mint of the Durotriges.

A predominantly British population continued to work the land and to live in the towns, with the addition of some 'Roman' landlords,

17

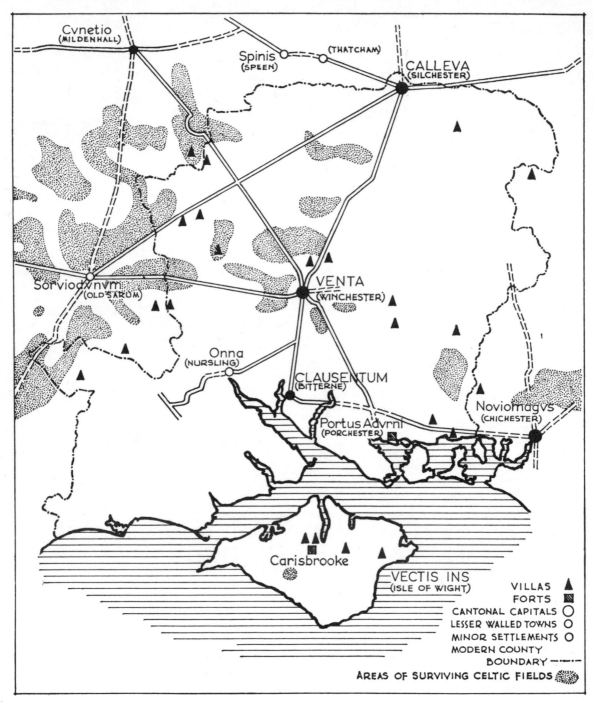

Legend:

VILLAS	▲
FORTS	▨
CANTONAL CAPITALS	◉
LESSER WALLED TOWNS	⦿
MINOR SETTLEMENTS	○
MODERN COUNTY BOUNDARY	— · —
AREAS OF SURVIVING CELTIC FIELDS	▨

Map labels:

Cvnetio (MILDENHALL)
Spinis (SPEEN)
(THATCHAM)
CALLEVA (SILCHESTER)
Sorviodvnvm (OLD SARUM)
VENTA (WINCHESTER)
Onna (NURSLING)
CLAUSENTUM (BITTERNE)
Portus Advrni (PORCHESTER)
Noviomagvs (CHICHESTER)
Carisbrooke
VECTIS INS (ISLE OF WIGHT)

Reproduced from the Ordnance Survey Map with the sanction of H.M. Stationery Office.
Crown Copyright reserved

Map 1. Roman Hampshire

many government officials, and some retired soldiers, as well as the garrison troops. The land was worked from a number of farmsteads. Certain 'villas' were apparently official centres of large government farming enterprises. There are large stock enclosures at Rockbourne and Damerham, and that great authority on Roman Britain, R. G. Collingwood, believed that the existence of a government weaving mill at *Venta Belgarum,* making cloth for the army, indicated widespread official sheep-farming on the Hampshire downs, replacing the corn grown in Celtic times.

Sparsholt mosaic

Other villas were just pleasant and smaller country houses for wealthy Romano-British gentlemen. There were a number of these small villas in the Isle of Wight, though the most famous villa there is the large composite group at Brading, including a bath block and domestic buildings with very fine mosaic pavements. On the mainland the important villa at Rockbourne, near Fordingbridge, has only recently been partially excavated. It stands in the midst of good farming land, was perhaps an important stock centre, and was lived in, though not continuously, until the end of the Roman occupation. Its many rooms include a 'red room' with a floor of tesserae in swastika pattern, and walls decorated with Pompeian red plaster and a grey and black dado. Many other villas cluster round Andover and Winchester. West Wood (Sparsholt), Grateley, Fullerton, Longstock and Abbott's Ann, have all been excavated and belong to the later years of the occupation. To the fourth century A.D. also belongs Lodge Farm, near North Warnborough, an earlier homestead, not on the direct line of any known Roman highway, which was turned into the bath-house of a simple 'villa' perhaps occupied by farm servants or other humble Romano-British folk. It was large, but its wattle partitions and chalk floors suggest that it was occupied by farm hands or domestic staff. These houses were probably in private ownership. Of course not all the owners were 'Roman', some were Romanised Britons. The Romanisation of British life began when Agricola was governor of Britain (A.D. 77–84), perhaps with government backing, though the majority of the native inhabitants continued to live squalidly and simply in huts. Some made use of the new and improved type of pottery produced by many Roman kilns in the New Forest. The villagers of Stockbridge Down possessed a few luxuries such as imitation Samian bowls. Though the conquerors brought a new coinage (there was perhaps a mint at *Clausentum*) Celtic coins continued to be the currency of the more backward part of the county.

A greatly improved road system was a more obvious and material result of the coming of the Romans. The roads probably date from

19

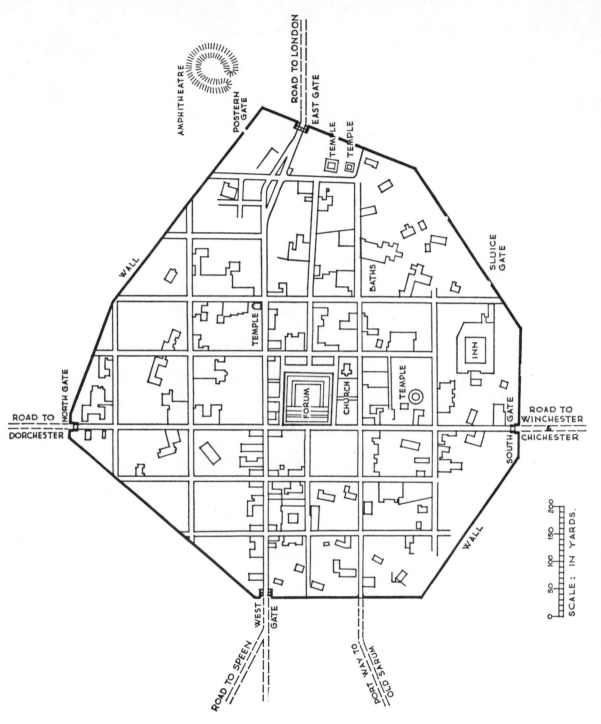

Map 2. Simplified Plan of *Calleva Atrebatum* (Silchester)

the early years of the occupation; military need rather than trade was the reason for their construction. *Venta Belgarum* (Winchester) was an important focal point in the system. How far, if at all, the city had been developed as a Belgic market town before the invasion is as yet impossible to say though there is much evidence of pre-Roman habitation around it, on St. Catherine's Hill, on Hockley Down, and on the western down of St. Paul's Hill. The site of *Venta* is still a flourishing and occupied part of modern Winchester, and excavation has therefore been only of a limited nature. Enough has been done to show that there were large and important buildings in the centre of the city and that part of the city wall is Roman in origin. The site of the government weaving mill has not yet been discovered.

In contrast to Winchester, *Calleva Atrebatum* (Silchester) is the only Roman town in England to be fully excavated. The whole of *Calleva* was laid out on a grid system of roads whose sides were crowded with shops, houses and administrative offices. There can be no doubt that this town played an important part in the Romanisation of northern Hampshire. Some of its bricks bear an official Neronian stamp. Recent re-excavation has confirmed the existence at *Calleva* of England's only Christian church of the Roman occupation, a building small in size when compared with the town's pagan temples, forum, public baths and rest house for the Imperial post.

In the later years of the Roman occupation, when Saxon pirates were already active, Roman settlements and ports on the Hampshire coast played their part as defences against the invaders. The great fortification of Portchester still remains, with its walls and bastions. A shore-fort at Carisbrooke helped to defend the Isle of Wight. The port of *Clausentum* was at first fortified by a simple wooden stockade across its peninsula (A.D. 120–150). A late stone wall suggests that its defences were reconstructed by order of Count Theodosius, Civil Governor of Britain in A.D. 368. Yet despite the potential strength of the coastal fortifications once the decision was taken to withdraw the Roman army, the fate of Hampshire and of Britain was settled. A new era of history began with the *Adventus Saxonum*, the coming of the Saxons.

Tradition and archaeology both suggest that Christianity first reached Hampshire in the Roman period. It is probable that the faith came with the traders who crossed the Channel in the wake of the army rather than with the army itself, where Emperor worship and the cult of Mithras were formidable rivals to Christianity. British bishops were present at the Council of Arles in 315, and about 100 years later the Pelagian heresy was rife in southern England, a heresy combated by the preaching of St. Germanus of Auxerre who is said to have landed

Bronze coin, Diocletian, A.D. 284–305

21

*Inscribed Roman ring
from Silchester*

on the Hampshire coast between Portsmouth and Southampton and healed the son of the leading man of the region, a tradition which suggests that Christianity, for a short while at least survived the withdrawal of the Roman army. A gold ring found at Silchester in 1786 inscribed with a common Christian formula, a small lead seal or stamp with a Christian monogram (formed from the Greek letters Chi and Rho) from the same town, and the small Christian church near *Calleva's* 'forum' are the only archaeological traces of Christianity in Roman Hampshire.

When the conversion of Hampshire began again in the seventh century, the inhabitants were said to be heathen. This disappearance of Christianity was perhaps significant; Romano-British civilisation did not prove to be a permanent foundation for the future development of Hampshire.

III The Coming of the Saxons and the Conversion of Hampshire to Christianity

In the second half of the third century southern England was again troubled by invaders from across the sea. The English historian, Bede, whose *History of the English Church and People* was completed in A.D. 731 calls these invaders Angles, Saxons and Jutes. Though Bede was a northerner, writing at Jarrow, he took great care to make his account of what happened in the south as accurate as possible and specifically says that he consulted his friend, Daniel, Bishop of Winchester from 705 until 744, about the early history of the diocese.

The new invaders were of Germanic origin, and can be conveniently referred to here as Saxons, for though the Angles gave their name to the country as a whole, certain Saxon groups established themselves in parts of England henceforth called after them, amongst them the West-Saxons of Wessex, which includes Hampshire, though much of the present county, parts of the New Forest and the Isle of Wight were settled by Jutes. Because of these invasions the Romans called the south-east coast of England the Saxon Shore. They were forced to increase its garrisons and its fortifications, and special sea patrols reported the movement of pirate vessels. Yet the invaders continued their raids, and when invasions by barbarians in other parts of the Roman Empire forced the Romans to withdraw their troops from England a period of confusion and uncertainty followed. The most reliable accounts of what happened in England when the Romans left are to be found in Bede and in the great *Anglo-Saxon Chronicle*, but neither Bede nor those who wrote down the traditions of their forefathers in the *Chronicle* were contemporary with the events they describe and the writers of the *Chronicle* were perhaps anxious to please the kings whose Saxon ancestors had carried out the conquest of England. According to the *Chronicle*, the conquest of Hampshire began in A.D. 495, when a Saxon warrior chief, Cerdic, and his son, Cynric (probably really his grandson) landed from a small fleet of ships at *Cerdicesora,* a place which was probably somewhere on the New Forest side of Southampton Water. Cerdic was the ancestor of the royal house of Wessex, whose activities form an important part of the *Chronicle*. By A.D. 530 he and his followers had conquered the Isle of Wight which he is said to have given to his 'kinsmen', Stuf and Whitgar in 534, the year in which he died.

Archaeological evidence suggests that the Jutes were prominent in the settlement of both the mainland and of the Island. At Chessel Down in the Island, excavations carried out between 1816 and 1855 recovered more than 130 Jutish graves, amongst them that of a warrior chieftain whose body had been prepared for burial with a veil or band, decorated with gold thread, covering his forehead; an iron girdle; silver gilt brooches; near his hand a dark wine-coloured crystal ball, probably contained in a silver gilt spoon. An earlier landing, at Portsmouth, was also probably Jutish. The *Chronicle* records that in 501, Port and his sons, Bieda and Maegla, came there with two ships and killed a British nobleman. The Jutes, too, conquered the valley of the River Meon; at Droxford, a large Jutish cemetery has produced grave goods of various kinds, swords, spearheads, shields and bosses. In eastern Hampshire the invaders were clearly able to make good use of the Meon River, following its valley inland, as Saxon bands followed the valley of the Test and of the Itchen. The invaders' movements towards the west may have been halted in about A.D. 552 by a British stand at what is now Old Sarum, but there appears to have been little organised opposition to the bands of invading Saxon raiders. The conquest of Hampshire was piecemeal and those Britons who tried to resist were either killed, captured as slaves, or driven farther westwards to the eventual isolation of Wales and of Cornwall. Romano-British civilisation·could offer little that was acceptable to the rough and illiterate warrior bands, and though there were skilled craftsmen amongst them, in general the Saxon invaders either destroyed or avoided the villas and towns of Roman Hampshire and *Calleva* was deserted.

When the initial period of conquest came to an end, the Saxons settled in new villages which had grown up along the river valleys, and a trading settlement began to develop at the mouth of the Itchen. The revival of town life did not occur, however, until the later Saxon period, and the main peacetime occupation of early Hampshire Anglo-Saxons was farming, the growing of barley for food and drink, and the slow clearance of forest land, though the area of the New Forest remained virtually uninhabited. The usual distinctions of society divided men into those of noble birth and those who worked on the land as freemen, ceorls, or as serfs.

What happened to *Venta Belgarum* is not yet known, but the city is ringed with pagan Saxon cemeteries and burials at Worthy Park, Micheldever, Winnall and on St. Giles Hill. Saxons buried on St. Giles Hill with their iron spearheads, knives, swords and shields, must have been a real threat to the Roman city below, but the evidence from excavation at Worthy Park does not suggest that the Winchester area was of much importance to the early Saxons, and indeed it has been called a cultural backwood. The splendid hanging bowl found in a burial in a Romano-British earthwork at Oliver's Battery shows the high standard of art which could be reached, but it is very unusual.

Hanging Bowl from Oliver's Battery

It was the conversion of Wessex which reintroduced civilisation to Hampshire, though Christianity made slow progress. Jewellery found in Winnall II is very beautiful, but the evidence of the 45 'Christian' graves found there show a community still hesitating to bury its dead near the living, still burying with grave goods, perhaps in propitiation of the old gods. A superb necklace of gold, garnets, silver, glass, ivory and bronze found in a burial in Lower Brook Street in 1971 may have belonged to a Winchester Christian and can certainly be regarded as a portent for the future and that high standard of Christian art which was going to be Anglo-Saxon Hampshire's great contribution to the western world.

In this society the most important personage was the warrior king, whose wandering existence was a result of his chief duty, the leading of his people to war. This the pagan kings of the West Saxons did with much success and when they and their people were converted to Christianity the resulting alliance between Church and State helped to secure Wessex's supremacy over the other Anglo-Saxon kingdoms. The conversion of Hampshire to Christianity was begun in A.D. 634 by St. Birinus, to whose mission there is a brief reference in Bede, in the *Anglo-Saxon Chronicle* and in a number of 'lives' of the Saint composed hundreds of years after his task was accomplished. Bede, an Englishman, whose chief complaint about the conquered Britons was their refusal to try to convert the pagan Saxons, described Birinus as converting the Geweissae (or West Saxons), who were completely heathen, and this may well mean that Christianity had disappeared from Hampshire after the withdrawal of the Romans. Birinus, according to one authority, was a Roman priest who was commissioned by Pope Honorius I to preach Christianity in those parts of England which had not received the Gospel. He may have landed at Portchester, was certainly kindly received by the King of the West Saxons, Cynegils, and in A.D. 635 baptized him, a very important event indeed, but one not followed by the conversion of all the royal family. Cynegil's second son, his successor, Cenwealh, was not yet a baptized Christian when he began to build the great church called the Old Minster in Winchester in 642. Three years later he was temporarily driven out of his kingdom by Penda of Mercia and was baptized only in 646 when in exile at the court of his Christian host, King Anna of the East Angles. According to the *Chronicle,* the conversion of the Isle of Wight followed that of the mainland, but it was the work of a missionary priest, Eoppa,

The baptism of Cynegils by St. Birinus

25

undertaken at the request of the exiled Bishop Wilfrid of Northumbria. In the same year the Island was 'harried' by Penda's Christian son, Wulfhere, who gave it to his godson, the king of the South Saxons.

In the early years of the Christian Church in Hampshire Birinus as bishop ruled a diocese which had its centre at Dorchester-on-Thames. Cenwealh divided this large diocese when he fell out with Bishop Agilbert and appointed Wini as bishop of the West Saxons, and Winchester began to be not just a royal city but the centre of the diocese. The bishop's chair ceased to be in Dorchester and Bishop Haeddi, in *c*. 676, brought Birinus's body to Winchester, the first of many such relics of English saints revered in the Old Minster. The close connection of the bishops with the royal family of Wessex undoubtedly made easier the work of conversion in Hampshire, yet it was a long time before every Hampshire village had its own church. The Gospel was probably preached from free-standing preaching crosses, of which fragments of only a few remain, and the Christian community was served by groups of priests working from fairly large churches known as 'Mynsters'. There was a Minster at Wic (near Southampton), a Minster at Twynham (Christchurch), a Minster at Wimborne on the edge of the New Forest, and a minster for nuns as well as the Cathedral Minster in Winchester, where Edward the Elder carried out the wish of his father, Alfred, by adding yet a third royal foundation, the New Minster, St. Frimbald's Abbey, consecrated in 903. Though it was a great part of Alfred's life work to re-establish Christian learning after the ravages of the Danes, a further revival and re-establishment was necessary by the middle of the 10th century. Bishop Ethelwóld (963–984), a monk himself, replaced the secular priests of the Old and New Minsters by monks of the reformed Cluniac Benedictine order, and virtually refounded and re-endowed the two Hampshire Benedictine nunneries of Romsey and St. Mary's, Winchester. Many of the early bishops were monks, but parish priests were not always celibate. Generous royal gifts of relics, money and landed endowments either directly to the various monastic houses, or the diocesan bishops, soon helped to turn the Anglo-Saxon Church in Hampshire into one of the wealthiest and largest dioceses in England; at first, the diocese was very large indeed, but by the reign of Edward the Elder, the creation of other sees reduced the area subject to the Bishops of Winchester and the diocese consisted, more or less, of the present counties of Surrey and Hampshire.

St. Swithun.
Headbourne Worthy

IV Anglo-Saxon Hampshire

The conversion of Anglo-Saxon England to Christianity was not followed by a period of peace or by political unity. For many years the country was harassed by internal wars and political power varied with the personality and military success of the local kings. In the eighth century the great central kingdom of Mercia became very strong, but after the death of Offa of Mercia in A.D. 796 Wessex became the leading kingdom, and its kings united England and drove back the new invaders, men from Scandinavia, usually called Danes or Vikings. Wessex had powerful neighbours, but King Egbert, who died in A.D. 839, succeeded in annexing Kent, was overlord of Mercia, harried Cornwall, and was recognised as Bretwalda, 'ruler of the British'. When southern England was again troubled by invaders in the middle of the ninth century, it was Egbert's son, Ethelwulf, and the most famous of his grandsons, Alfred, who organised the opposition and eventually drove back the Danes. After Alfred made peace with the Danes in A.D. 877 and their leader Guthrum was baptised, many Danes remained in England in the area known as the Danelaw, but Alfred's military successes made possible the blossoming of Anglo-Saxon civilisation, and established the political importance of Wessex.

Penny of Ethelwulf, struck in Hampshire

The kingdom of Wessex consisted of a number of shires, and the historic existence of Hampshire goes back to at least A.D. 757. In that year, according to the *Anglo-Saxon Chronicle,* King Sigberht, who had ruled badly, was deprived of most of his kingdom except for 'Hamtun-scire'. The shire presumably derives its name from Hamtun, the Anglo-Saxon settlement in the south of the county and the predecessor of the medieval town of Southampton. Significantly it was not called after the centre of the diocese, Winchester (*Wintanceaster*) though that cathedral city later became the county town. By the time of Alfred, local government in Hampshire, as in other Wessex shires, was the responsibility of an official known as an ealdorman who also had to lead the men of his shire in time of war as did the ealdorman Wulfheard who routed the Danish attack on Southampton in A.D. 840. Ealdormen were royal officials, sometimes members of the royal family, but they often had their own local estates, and their local knowledge was of help when they administered the King's laws and presided over the shire's court. At least one ealdorman of Wessex, Aelfric, had his own personal

The Seal of Aelfric

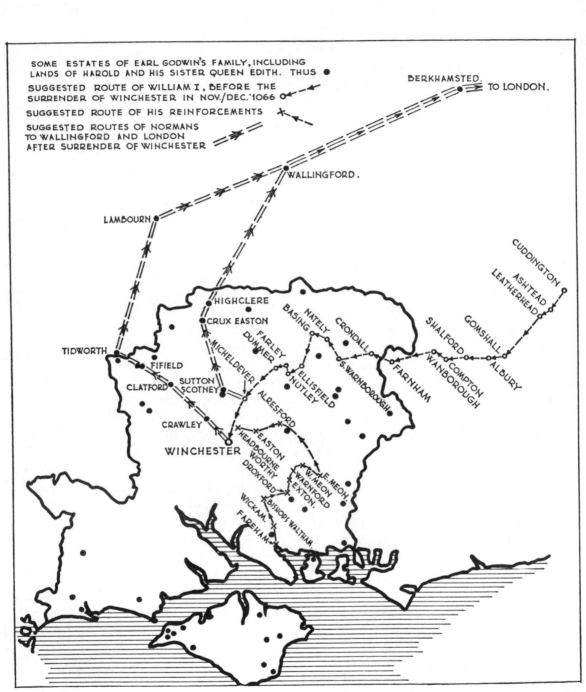

Map 3. Hampshire estates of the Godwin family *c.* 1065 and possible route of the Norman army.

seal; it was he who betrayed the army to the Danes in 992 and again in 1003 and who was killed at Ashingdon in 1016.

Much of what is known of Anglo-Saxon society is derived from the various codes of laws compiled by successive kings of Wessex and political history is contained in the *Anglo-Saxon Chronicle,* a great chronological record written down in the vernacular, of which the earliest surviving manuscript has a particular Hampshire interest, for much of it was written in Winchester, probably in the Old Minster. The use of the Anglo-Saxon language for codes of law and for the writing of history did much to encourage the feeling that England under the leadership of the royal house of Wessex was becoming a nation, and the feeling of national pride was encouraged by Alfred's successes against the Danes, by the growth of English towns, and by a revival and reorganisation within the national Church.

In Hampshire it is clear that there were important towns at Southampton and at Winchester. The centre which gave the shire its name, Hamtun, was not on the site of the later medieval and present town, but appears to have been composed of two districts on the peninsula of land lying between the Rivers Test and Itchen. It has been suggested that the prefix 'South' was added to distinguish two parts of the settled area from each other, and not to distinguish the town from Northampton in another county. On the Test side perhaps stood Hamtun, but its site has not been identified. On the shores of a lagoon formed by the Itchen stood Hamwic, the commercial area of the town, perhaps as its name may suggest, a trading suburb of the fortified main settlement. Hamwic had a Minster church, the 'Minister at Wic' being the original of the church later dedicated to St. Mary, the mother church of modern Southampton. Hamwic, described as a *Mercimonium,* was convenient for trade with the Continent, and recent archaeological excavations have resulted in the discovery of jars and flagons for wine-carrying, and fine imported glassware. Yet its position was very vulnerable; Ealdorman Wulfheard was able to defeat a Viking attack on Hamwic in 840, but in 980 a very severe raid resulted in the slaughter or captivity of most of the population.

The Viking raids on Southampton, and the fact that the bishop's Chair was at Winchester were both factors which helped to increase the importance of the cathedral city. Yet very little indeed is known of Winchester as an Anglo-Saxon centre before the reign of Edward the Confessor. Like Southampton, it was a *burh,* or fortified centre to be defended against the Danes, a place of resistance and refuge in time of trouble. The system is described in a document called the Burghal Hidage, dating from the reign of Edward the Elder—though the idea

King Alfred the Great, statue in Winchester

29

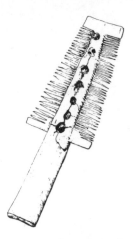

Saxon comb from Hamwic

probably originated with his father Alfred, and listing the centres which were to be fortified and the number of men required to man them. In Hampshire there were *burhs* at Winchester, Southampton, Twynham and in the Roman port of Portchester, the last a late addition to the system. A recent interpretation of the Winchester evidence suggests that the fortification of the *burh* coincides with the line of the Roman-medieval wall and needed some 2,400 men to man its total length of nearly two miles. All that can be added with any degree of certainty of Winchester in the hundred years after Alfred's death is that the layout of the town was dominated by two factors. The group of three royally-founded minster churches already referred to occupied much of the area on the south side of the High Street, and secondly, the presence of the river Itchen and of many brooks was an important factor in the topography of the city. It is also reasonable to assume that the Anglo-Saxon kings had some sort of residence in Winchester and that their hall or palace was not far from the three minsters. There were undoubtedly other royal 'residences' within the county, for example perhaps at Andover, where Edgar made part of his Law, and where Ethelred the Unready stood as sponsor to Olaf of Norway in 994 in a period of temporary peace with the Danish invaders, and perhaps also at Twynham, where there was a 'residence'.

Later on, for a short period in the first half of the 11th century England was ruled by Danish kings, a period of considerable growth and prosperity in Hampshire. Cnut, his wife Emma (widow of Ethelred the Unready) and their son Hardicanute were all buried in the Old Minster at Winchester, one of the many Anglo-Saxon foundations enriched by the Danish royal family in England. In 1043 the old line of English kings was restored by the coronation in Winchester cathedral of Edward the Confessor, the son of Emma by her first marriage.

It was a measure of the vitality and integrity of Anglo-Saxon civilisation that it was able to withstand and even in some ways to profit from the prolonged struggles with the Danes. To this civilisation Hampshire made an important and considerable contribution. The two royal monasteries at Winchester became the fountain heads of a moving and magnificent style of manuscript illumination and writing which is now known all over the civilised world as the 'Winchester School'. Its most famous example is the Benedictional of St. Ethelwold, commissioned by that bishop and known to have been at Hyde Abbey (Newminster) in the later medieval period, though it may have been made in the Old Minster or indeed in one of the monasteries outside Hampshire reformed by Bishop Ethelwold's influence. The great minster churches themselves were renowned examples of contemporary architecture, richly decorated and famous for their music. Indeed, their outstanding contribution to England's musical history, the Winchester 'tropes', ornamental additions to plainsong music which went out of fashion after 1066, can be recalled today from the existence of two rare manuscripts, the Winchester trophers. A less formal kind of music was envisaged in the special provision which the church made for the particularly English custom of pealing bells, provision confirmed at the great national synod held in Winchester in *c.* 970, a synod which apparently met at Bishop Ethelwold's request and issued the *Regularis Concordia,* an agreed rule for general use in all English monasteries.

The language of the Church was Latin, which was also often used for some formal documents and charters concerning land. Yet the language of the ordinary people was alive and already so strong in use that it was able to survive the Norman Conquest, to conquer French, and emerge at the end of the Middle Ages as the language of English society. Its strength was helped by the translations of King Alfred, by the continued existence of the *Chronicle,* by the fact that Anglo-Saxon was used in many charters and official documents, and that it was also the language of some serious scholarhip. Wulfstan of Winchester wrote descriptive poems about his monastery and its music; Alfric the Grammarian (*c.* 980–*c.* 1020) compiled vast quantities of original homilies for feast days, lives of saints, and sermons for all occasions.

The civilisation of Anglo-Saxon Christian Hampshire was thus vigorous and manifold and was never insular nor merely local. Trade with Western Europe flourished, and with Scandinavia, the Anglo-Saxon Church, though it had its peculiarities, was part of Christendom. It was a monk from Nursling, near Southampton, St. Boniface, who, in a series of great missionary journeys, preached Christianity to the Frisians before his martyrdom at their hands in 754. Boniface had the help and encouragement of the Bishop of Winchester, Daniel, and of the Pope; regular contacts were always maintained with the Papal Curia. There were frequent contacts, too, with France; the first Abbot of Newminster, St. Grimbald, was a Frenchman. Emma, mother of Edward the Confessor, sister of Duke Richard of Normandy and 'the Gem of the Normans', spent much of her widowhood at Wherwell and in Winchester after the death of her second husband, Cnut. When her son, Edward the Confessor, was crowned King of England in Winchester cathedral in 1043, Winchester was no longer merely the chief town in Wessex, but had become the royal capital of Anglo-Saxon England.

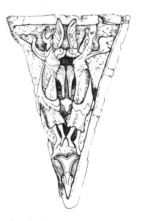

Anglo-Saxon angels, ivory carving, St. Cross

31

V The Hampshire Domesday: (i) The County in the Reign of Edward the Confessor 1043-66

In the 11th century the office of ealdorman of the county declined in importance. Instead, the most importmant layman in Hampshire was the Earl (*comes*) of Wessex, a nobleman with great estates who left the routine work of administration to his deputy (*vice-comes*) the shire reeve (sheriff) of Hampshire. In the reign of Edward the Confessor (1043–66) the most powerful man of Wessex was Earl Godwin, whose daughter Edith married the king, and whose second son, Harold, was the famous last Anglo-Saxon king of England. Twenty years after Harold's defeat and death at Hastings, William the Conqueror caused to be compiled his great Domesday Survey. 'Domesday Book' consists of two volumes of which the smaller, 'Little Domesday', is concerned only with East Anglia; the larger survey covers all the other counties, including Hampshire. This survey is of paramount importance in the history of the county for its object was to furnish detailed information of the financial and economic condition of Hampshire not only as it was in 1086, but as it had been at the end of the reign of the Confessor, 'On the day when King Edward was alive and dead', and also to note the value of landed estates if and when they had been re-granted by King William earlier in his reign. The plan of the Inquiry is very simple. Hampshire was surveyed under the names of the great owners of land, including the king himself; within each personal estate thus described the county was further divided into Hundreds. Each Hundred had its own ancient name and its own local court, and within each Hundred the basic holding was the manor, which varied in size and in the geld which it paid. Though this division is not without difficulty and meant, for example, that in order to construct a picture of any particular Hundred, the whole survey had to be used, the record as a whole is complete and efficient, the greatest single achievement of all early English administration. When it was finished it was kept in the Treasury at Winchester, by royal command. The king's instructions to his Commissioners has survived, and it is clear from their orders and from the results of their work that they were required to obtain as detailed an account of each manor as was possible, who the inhabitants were, if they paid geld direct to the king or if it was paid

9. St. Thomas' Church, Winchester (Architect, 1845–1857, E. W. Elmslie). Now the Hampshire County Record Office.

10. Old St. Thomas' Church: water-colour by G. F. Prosser.

11.   The Nave, Winchester Cathedral, looking west.

by the lord of the manor, how much land there was, whether it was wooded or meadow, or pasture, if there was a mill and if there was a church. This survey of manors and their holders thus provides the social and economic basis of the essential political feudalism by which the Conqueror ruled his kingdom. All the information was supplied by juries from each Hundred, and other men, too, the sheriff of the county, reeves, priests, who gave additional evidence on oath if required to do so.

In the Hampshire of Edward the Confessor, the king himself was the most important landed proprietor, and his most important separate estate was the city of Winchester, where his position in some respects was that of general landlord to the burgesses of the city. Their distinctive burgess tenure was essentially their free right to let and to sell their freehold property provided they gave due notice in the borough court. Property held by burgess tenure in this way paid the king a 'gablum', a rent for each house-gable, and the duty of paying gablum passed with the property from owner to owner. It was still being assessed in Winchester in the 18th century, as tarrage. Edward the Confessor obtained this rent from 63 burgesses, but this information is not in Domesday Book. Winchester, the capital of England, was probably too large a town to fit into the general survey and, like London, was left out. Special surveys of the town made in 1110 and 1148, bound together in one volume, the so-called Winchester Domesday, make good this earlier deficiency. On the eve of the Norman Conquest Winchester was a flourishing city. On the north side of the High Street stood two halls of 'Chenictes', gilds of knights whose function was perhaps to defend the city. The eastern hall can be identified as the later St. John's House; the other, western, hall was on a site which was fronted by shops belonging to Newminster, approached by a lane off the High Street, at the rear of the building which is now No. 85 High Street. Near the Westgate was a house which belonged to the king's consort, Godwin's daughter, farther down the High Street were the minters and moneyers, makers of the king's coin, the money of England, Aelfwine, Aitwardesonne, Alestan and Andrebod, as well as Godwin Socche, the master moneyer. Local government in Winchester was still very much controlled by the frequent presence of the king, but its beginning is indicated by the mention of Winchester reeves and street beadles. This information and much else about Anglo-Saxon Winchester is to be found in the earlier of the two Winchester surveys, which compares the town as it was in 1110 with what it had been in the time of King Edward. To it may be added some occasional references which occur in Domesday Book proper, when the city is mentioned because certain county landowners have financial interests in it, for example the Abbess of Wherwell who had a mill and 31 messuages, and the Abbess of Romsey who also had burgesses in Winchester.

Though the other boroughs of Twynham and Southampton are both individually described in the Survey of 1086, the account given of them is very scanty. Perhaps Hamtun was still on its early Anglo-Saxon site, and not fully recovered from its sacking of 980. Yet its burgesses, apparently 76 in number, paid £7 gablum to the king. The rebuilding of the town may have been begun in Cnut's time, in an area now represented by the medieval walled town. The mother church remained the minster at South Stoneham.

In the country generally King Edward's royal demesne, the manors which he had not let to a tenant, varied in size and in value and were scattered over Hampshire and the Isle of Wight. He had land at Basingstoke, Hurstbourne, Andover, Wymering, Portchester, Rock-bourne, King's Somborne, Titchfield, and Twyford. His queen drew revenues from Anstey near Alton, Greatham, Selborne, Upton, Kingsclere, and Penton Grafton. Her father, the Earl of Wessex, and her brothers were all richly endowed with Hampshire revenues, but the Godwin fortunes varied with politics. The earl was banished for a short time in 1051 and though he was back at the king's table in 1053 his death in that year and at that table was considered by many to be a fit punishment for his alleged part in the murder of the king's brother, Alfred. The Winchester annalist compiling the chronicle which was kept in the Old Minster recorded the event with brevity, ' "May this crumb choke me," said Earl Godwin, "If I killed your brother" . . . and he died'. Godwin's second son, Harold, succeeded him as Earl of Wessex.

Amongst other prominent lay landowners were royal 'thegns' and courtiers. One of them, Odo de Winchestre, had property which included land in the Isle of Wight and at Chawton, and his brother Eldred was tenant at Micheldever of Newminster and of the Bishop of Winchester. Perhaps the most important of the thegns was Cheping of Worthy who had 14 manors as well as two houses in Winchester and three in Southampton.

The estates of lay owners might vary with political change. Manors owned by ecclesiastics were not usually subject to such political hazards and in Hampshire a fundamental and unchanging feature of the economy of the county even as recently as the mid-19th century was the large proportion of land, the many manors, owned by the Church. Chief amongst these ecclesiastical owners was the Bishop of Winchester himself. It was the wealth of the Anglo-Saxon bishopric which made it possible for Bishop Ethelwold to rebuild the cathedral church of the old monastery in Winchester, and for later, medieval, bishops

34

to make it a storehouse of countless treasures. It is not yet really clear at what historical point there occurred a main division of the bishop's property into those manors which provided the resources and revenue of the bishoprics and those which were for the 'support of the monks', that is, for the cathedral and priory church of St. Swithun in Winchester. The bishop's own manors and those of the priory made up the two major landed estates in the county, much of the land being of royal gift of considerable antiquity; of manor after manor it is recorded in Domesday that it belonged to the bishop or that it was always the minster's. Very few private donations are recorded, one interesting exception being the gift (to Newminster) of land at Tatchbury in Eling by the sheriff, Ezi, a gift made for King Edward's soul.

Romsey Abbey

Other Hampshire monasteries had smaller but also valuable estates, Newminster, the canons of Twynham, the nuns of St. Mary's (Winchester), Romsey, and Wherwell. Many of these ecclesiastical manors were kept in demesne, that is worked directly by the monastery concerned, through its own local lay officials; the minority were let to lay tenants at money rents, though rents in kind were not unknown. Newminster let Comer in Corhampton for the annual rent of wine, perhaps from grapes grown locally, especially since wine is produced today in nearby Hambledon. It is this aspect of Domesday, the use which it records of the land, which makes it so important as a source of Hampshire's social and economic history. Though the main unit was the manor, that term was applied in many different ways. The huge Priory manor of Chilcomb stretched for many miles round Winchester. Other manors were obviously smaller districts; some are said to have had halls, perhaps the predecessors of what were later and often wrongly called 'manor houses'. Thus there were two halls at Warnford, two at Clere, three at Knapp, in Christchurch, one at Portchester, with its own fishery, one at Boarhunt, with its own mill.

With the many mills and churches they formed the only permanent buildings in or near the poor and squalid hovels which made up the majority of buildings in Hampshire Anglo-Saxon villages. It is clear that there was much mixed farming and that rivers and forest played an important part in the county's economy. Forests were not merely waste places where the nobility could hunt; forest land fed swine and produced honey, timber and rough pasture for cattle. Hampshire's many rivers were also a valuable asset to those whose estates contained them. Hay, from water meadows, and fish, including eels, were only part of this riverside wealth and the production of flour, from differing kinds of grains, depended almost entirely on the existence of many rivers with water-mills.

VI The Hampshire Domesday: (ii) The Effect of the Norman Conquest

Christchurch Castle

East Meon church

Some few weeks after the battle of Hastings, Winchester surrendered to William the Conqueror, a submission apparently sent by Queen Edith, the Confessor's widow, who was living in the city. It is not absolutely certain when William I first came into Hampshire, but one of his first acts in Winchester was to demolish the houses of 12 burgesses and to build himself a palace in the centre of the High Street, on this site and on other land taken from Newminster. A Domesday jury noted that this latter part of the site was already royal property and that William had therefore no need to compensate the Abbey with other land at Kingsclere and at Alton. In any case, the life of this palace was short, for it appears to have been destroyed in the civil war of Stephen's reign, when the triumphant diocesan bishop, Henry de Blois, used the materials to rebuild his own palace-castle at Wolvesey. The site in the High Street was difficult to defend and by the reign of Henry II there was a royal fortress on the western hill, Winchester Castle, where the last Anglo-Saxon bishop of Winchester, Stigand, died as a prisoner in 1070. Even more majestic is the cathedral, a massive demonstration of the impact of the Conquest, for the first Norman bishop of the diocese, Walkelin, completely demolished the Anglo-Saxon church and his new building retains its Norman framework beneath later additions and alterations. The architectural and engineering skill of the Normans enabled them to construct a huge church on a very poor foundation, but the central tower soon collapsed and was replaced after 1100 by a second structure of much finer and more substantial masonry in the later Romanesque style. Simple round-headed arches, rounded columns, and lack of ornament and small slit windows are the significant features which distinguish the smaller Hampshire churches rebuilt in the Norman and Romanesque periods. Much of this building was done in Caen stone quarried in Normandy and imported to Hampshire via Southampton.

The power of the Normans and the military nature of the Conquest soon made itself felt all over the county. At Southampton a new royal castle was erected on a mound overlooking the western shore, for the town was an important embarkation point for kings whose dominions were on both sides of the English Channel. Southampton Castle was not only a strong point but it was also a royal storehouse, great quantities of wine being imported and kept in huge vaults within the castle precincts. Outside of these precincts the town grew rapidly on its new site, and according to Domesday Book, the population had very greatly increased by the Norman Conquest. To a total of some 70 to 80 burgesses of Anglo-Saxon origin was added 65 French- and

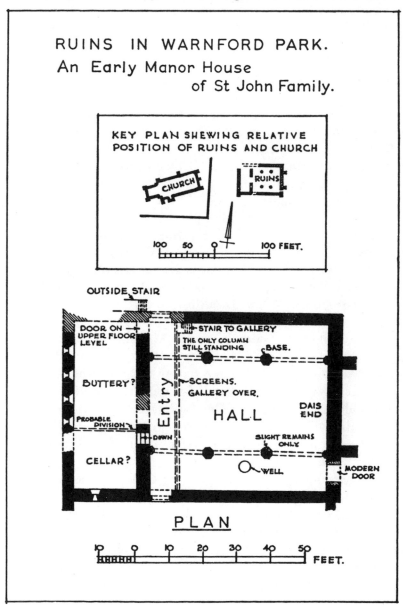

Map. 4. A manor house of the de Port, later St. John, family in Warnford Park

*Norman house,
Southampton*

31 English-speaking families, whose coming greatly increased the town's prosperity and whose presence also resulted in a linguistic division, for the main streets soon became known as French and English Streets. Many merchants in both Winchester and Southampton were probably bi-lingual, for a striking feature of town life in Hampshire at this time was the easy and frequent communication with French-speaking merchants from the other side of the Channel. By the first half of the 12th century there was a resident Jewish community in Winchester. As this community developed and grew in size its members maintained a close connection with Normandy, and the majority of Hampshire Jews in Southampton, in Romsey and in Portsmouth probably continued to speak French. Norman-French was the language of the great Norman — Plantaganet Civil Service, though Latin, the language of the Church, was much used for administrative records. The Hampshire peasant and the poorer townspeople continued to speak English, but there must have been many bi-lingual families.

The changes brought about by the Conquest were not confined to architecture and language. The most important effects on the county as a whole include the growth of town life in all its aspects, the development of a strong central government administration, and the handing over of estates to new Norman landowners. The development of Hampshire towns is considered in a later chapter, but here it may be noted that the Conquest had an immediate effect on Hampshire landlords. The power of Earl Godwin's family was broken, though his daughter, the Old Lady, Queen Edith, continued to live on in Winchester until her death in 1070. William I succeeded to the ancient demesne land of Edward the Confessor, and to these the Crown added other property by forfeiture or by death; the land of the 'Old Lady', estates from Bishop Stigand, and the Hampshire lands of the rebellious Earl Roger of Hereford. Only a few Hampshire thegns withstood the storm of the Conquest, amongst them Odo of Winchester, who lost land in the Isle of Wight and in Chawton, but who had acquired by 1086 five Hampshire houses which had previously belonged to other Englishmen in the reign of King Edward. Cheping of Worthy was not so fortunate, for the greater part of his estate was given to Ralf de Mortimer, though he may have been allowed a very small holding at Candover. By the time Domesday Book was written the greatest of the new Hampshire lay landlords was Hugh de Port, who was apparently a vassal of Bishop Odo of Bayeux. The Conqueror appointed him Sub-constable of Dover Castle, and as a part payment gave him the manor of Barfreston in Kent, where the wall paintings in the church used to depict scenes from Hugh's life, including his final years as a monk in St. Swithun's Priory in Winchester. The family

38

were undoubtedly devout. At Warnford in the Meon Valley, held by Hugh from the monks of Newminster, the church bears two original inscriptions recording its rebuilding by the de Ports, and Pamber Priory, near Basingstoke, was a de Port foundation.

Tomb of Richard of Beorn

In Hampshire Hugh held about 56 manors direct from the Crown, 13 as a tenant of the Bishop of Bayeux, a great 'fief' which had a long existence remaining intact for many years in the hands of his heirs, the de Ports and the St. Johns. This fief had its centre or *caput* at Basing, and the site has recently been acquired by the County Council, and is now open to the public. Like all the de Port houses, it was a fortified house, with a moat. Moated houses are unusual in Hampshire, and Basing was fortified again on a vast scale by the fifth Marquess of Winchester, and gained fame as 'Loyalty House', the centre of Royalist resistance during the Civil War.

One of the secondary residences of the de Port family was at Warnford and the ruined remnant of this building is a rare example in Hampshire of a great early medieval stone hall-house.

The Conqueror's grant to Newminster of land at Kingsclere and Alton has already been mentioned. He also gave that abbey an estate at Laverstoke for the sake of his soul and that of his queen, Matilda, and there is indeed no evidence, as has been suggested, that William disliked Newminster or tried to impoverish it. Not one of the old Anglo-Saxon monastic foundations suffered permanent loss of endowment as a result of the Conquest, and, moreover, certain important Norman monasteries were also endowed with Hampshire estates, Jumieges receiving land at Hayling Island, and Mont St. Michel the very rich living of Basingstoke. The bishopric of Winchester and the monks of the Cathedral Church continued to be exceptionally rich, and part of their incomes was used for the rebuilding of Winchester Cathedral and the construction of new and larger parish churches.

The Conqueror and his sons were frequently in Hampshire. William I continued the ancient custom, at least as old as Cnut's reign, of 'wearing his Crown' in Winchester at Eastertide: two of his sons, William Rufus and Richard of Beorn, were killed in the New Forest and both were buried in Winchester Cathedral. When Rufus died it was to Winchester that his brother and successor, Henry I, came, to make sure of the royal treasure, and it was from a Hampshire nunnery, Romsey, that he took his English wife, Edith, and thus united the line of the Anglo-Saxon and Norman royal families. After Henry I's death it was the military struggle for Winchester which became a vital point in the civil war between his daughter Matilda and her rival, Stephen de Blois, whose chief supporter was his brother Henry, Bishop of Winchester. Fierce and brutal though the civil war was, this period of anarchy

The Rufus Stone, New Forest

39

Round Table,
Great Hall,
Winchester Castle

at length paved the way for the return of strong government under Henry II.

The efficiency of the county's local government depended much on the services of able country gentlemen who were Sheriffs of Hampshire (see Chapter XVII), but this administration in turn depended wholly on the strength and ability of the monarch. Henry II destroyed or slighted the fortifications of adulterine, illegal, castles, including those of Henry de Blois, and future bishops of Winchester, though wealthy and influential, always remained loyal subjects of the kings. The arrangement by which the King's Judges went on circuit were improved and the Assize came regularly to Hampshire, and law and order was restored, reinforced by the actual presence of the kings in their great castle on Winchester's western hill, the embodiment of Norman and Angevin majesty. The castle was an important link in the chain of military defences in southern England, had a great keep, was surrounded by a strong wall and ditch, and its main gateway with drawbridge and portcullis was approached from the west. A secret Sally Port had tunnels leading city-wards, and was an unusual feature, but the great hall is now the only survival above ground, illustrating perfectly the splendour and the isolation of medieval kingship. There were private apartments and chapels too, but the great hall, begun by Rufus and perfected by Henry III under the direction of a master goldsmith, Elias of Dereham, and adorned since at least the 14th century by the Round Table is only equalled and not surpassed by that at Westminster. Here were held great feasts; great trials and important meetings of early parliaments. The building survived the great fire in the Castle in 1302, when Edward I and his second queen escaped from the royal apartments which were burnt out, but the royal finances were so bad that restoration was impossible, and later monarchs usually stayed at Wolvesey. The Assize continued to be held in the great hall, however, and in 1764 ugly partitioning was put up by order of the county justices to create two new court rooms. A major reconstruction was initiated in 1871 by the then chairman of Hampshire Quarter Sessions, Melville Portal, but new courts built nearby had to be demolished just before the Second World War, and the hall was once more used for Assizes, until the opening of the new Crown Courts by the then Lord Chancellor, Lord Hailsham, on 22 February 1974. Assizes were abolished, and the great hall is once more under extensive repair and renovation.

The majesty of early kings was displayed, too, in the cathedral on suitable occasions. Henry II had his eldest son, Henry, crowned in Winchester Cathedral as his successor, though the young king died soon afterwards. The great English-French empire held together, despite the

40

quarrels of the old king and his surviving sons, Richard and John, and Hampshire's importance within this empire was confirmed again on 17 April 1194 on Richard I's return from captivity at the end of his Crusade. A great procession led the king from castle to cathedral, the monks washed away his disgrace in a ceremonial bathing, Coeur de Lion once more wore the Crown of England in a long and splendid ceremony designed to impress and to re-establish the monarchy. Graced by the presence of the king's formidable mother, Eleanor of Aquitaine, it was the last great crown wearing in Hampshire.

The county has never lacked historians, and after the coming of the Normans, the professional writers of history were monks. One of the most distinguished of these chroniclers was William of Malmesbury who saw with his own eyes some of the great epic confrontations of the 12th-century civil wars, recorded in his *Historia Novella*, and other writings. Later on Richard of Devizes, a monk of St. Swithun's Priory, wrote a famous account of Richard I and his Crusade, and was also responsible for many entries in the year-by-year record kept in his great church. These *Annales Wintonie* are a basis for much local history, including the architectural development of the cathedral. Richard of Devizes was almost certainly an Englishman, Malmesbury of mixed Norman and English blood. Another chronicler, Geoffrey of Monmouth, was writing about the distant 'British' history and describing the exploits of King Arthur, whose Round Table was soon to adorn the great hall of the Kings of England in Winchester Castle. Though London was growing, Winchester remained a very important royal centre for the peripatetic Angevin monarchy, and John's son and heir, Henry III, was born in Winchester Castle in 1207. Portsmouth and Southampton, too, were important Norman-Plantagenet towns. Hampshire was on the route to France, and until John lost his French inheritance, the county was very much a part of Europe.

VII The Towns of Medieval Hampshire

The Moot Horn of City of Winchester

Though the towns of medieval Hampshire had certain problems in common, problems of constitutional growth and of the development of local government, each flourishing community was also very different from the other, illustrating in many ways the differing social and economic aspects of civic life. The Sheriff of the county was not normally popular in Hampshire towns and there was a general wish to exclude him, though his power was strong and his duties of preserving law and order and collecting royal revenue through town bailiffs gave him frequent opportunities for interfering in municipal affairs. With the king's consent the Sheriff could be excluded from towns which obtained permission to collect the royal revenues and make their own financial returns to the Exchequer as a fixed rent or 'farm'. This right, to return the farm, was granted by royal charter; when it was a grant in perpetuity, known as a 'fee-farm', a very important stage in local constitutional development had been reached.

The movement towards independence was encouraged by the diminution of royal authority in the troubles of Stephen's reign (1135–54), by the need to encourage urban revival in the particular cases of Winchester and Andover, both of which were burnt and pillaged in the civil war, and by the examples of certain French towns where the townspeople formed themselves into 'communes', headed by an officer known as the mayor. In some Hampshire towns this commune or commonalty led the movement towards independence. In other towns it was the Merchant Gild (a group of influential and wealthy townsmen which regulated trade and also met regularly for social and commercial reasons) which formed a nucleus of opposition to the Sheriff and obtained charters of privileges from the king. These are such important points that it is worthwhile examining them in the light of what actually happened in certain particular towns.

Arms of City of Winchester

In Southampton the right of the gildsmen to form their own gild as they had done in the time of Henry I was confirmed by Henry II in 1154. Yet the charter of 1199 given by King John granted the fee-farm of the town, with that of Portsmouth, to the townsmen 'our men of Southampton', not to the gildsmen. The fee-farm was then fixed at the annual rent of £200. The first mention of a mayor of Southampton occurs before 1221, and a little later on, probably in

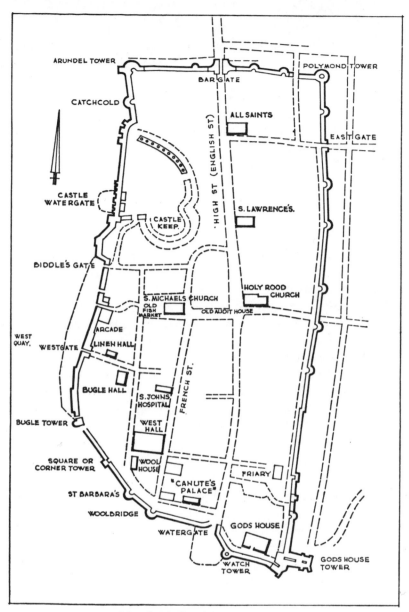

Map 5. Medieval Southampton.

1230, a certain Benedict Ace became mayor. He apparently held office for a long period, but in October 1249 the townspeople obtained a promise from Henry III that they should never again be governed by a mayor. For some years Southampton was again ruled by bailiffs, until 1267–8 when the Alderman of the gild was the chief officer. For the next 50 or 60 years the gild's was the chief voice in Southampton affairs, and the regular succession of mayors did not begin until 1333.

43

It was satisfactory for towns when they were able, by returning their own fee-farm, to exclude the Sheriff of the county from their financial affairs, but he could still interfere to enforce the king's writs. Southampton reached a further stage of independence in 1447 when the town, by royal charter, became 'the county of the town of Southampton', with its own Sheriff, as well as mayor, and therefore with the right to make returns of writs direct to the king himself or to his judicial officers. For this reason, Southampton enjoys a unique position in the later history of Hampshire towns: there is still a Sheriff who is always the mayor of the town in the year following his election as Sheriff.

Inland from Southampton, the town of Andover had markedly similar constitutional characteristics, the earliest Andover charter being a grant to the Gild Merchant there by Henry II in 1175-6, confirmed by John in 1201 on payment of 20 marks and a palfrey. There are many later confirmations and, unlike Southampton, a very fine series of gild records which make a unique contribution to the county's medieval history, producing the most complete surviving account of a Merchant Gild from any Hampshire town. The Andover records show the gild to have been divided into two 'houses', an upper house, the 'free' gild, a lower house or veillein or hanse gild. Regular meetings were held to appoint new members, make trade regulations and elect bailiffs. The bailiff's chief duty was to preside over an independent local court, dealing with the two districts into which Andover was divided, 'in hundred' and 'out hundred'. There was no mayor and no commune.

It is a significant fact that in these two towns, Andover and Southampton, where the power of the gild for so long a period was so important, the majority of the inhabitants depended directly upon commerce for their livelihoods. Southampton was a port, with a flourishing wine trade with France, and a varied coastal trade. Andover's importance in the medieval county was in the wool trade, for which the neighbouring Weyhill Fair was an important distribution centre. During the 13th century the wool trade was probably more important than the actual making of cloth, though cloth making was the subject of many regulations continually made by the gild.

Only three other Hampshire towns are known with certainty to have had Merchant Gilds besides those at Andover and Southampton, and in these, the towns of Petersfield, Portsmouth, and Winchester, the pattern of constitutional development was different, the gild privileges and customs of Winchester being used as a model for the other two centres. Petersfield was a manorial borough, belonging to William, Earl of Gloucester, but its burgesses were free enough to gain in Henry II's reign the right of having a Merchant Gild on the model of that of Winchester. In Winchester the townspeople held their property as burgesses, with the right to dispose of their real estate as they wished without having to obtain permission from an overlord, and subject only to certain formalities in the city court. There was a Gild Merchant at least as early as the reign of Henry I, but the nucleus of free government was also certainly to be found in the essential freedoms of burgess tenure, and the fact that a city court had to meet regularly. By 1155, there would appear to have been two groups in the city both able to negotiate charters from Henry II, who made one grant to his citizens of Winchester confirming their ancient privileges, and another to members of the Gild Merchants, including freedom from toll. A mayor of Winchester is referred to in 1200, but the Gild Merchant remained the most powerful group in civic affairs until about 1278. Though for a short period in 1155 the Winchester *prepositus* or reeve, Stigand, accounted for the city's farm direct to the Exchequer and not via the sheriff, it was perhaps difficult for a city whose townspeople were much dependent economically on the frequent presence of the king and his sheriff to sustain a continuous demand to manage its own financial affairs. Not until 1327 did Winchester obtain the right to return its fee-farm. Membership of the Winchester Gild remained the nominal way, but a formal way only, of becoming a freeman of the city until the reform of the Corporation in 1835. The earliest surviving copy of Winchester's local laws and trade regulations, the Usages, was probably compiled in about 1278 after some months of disturbance and obvious dissension between the gild and non-gildsmen members of the Winchester Commune, and embodies many earlier customs and traditions. The gild had become a mere social club and in contrast to Andover, it was the Corporation of Winchester, the Commonalty of Twenty-Four led by a mayor who regulated the all-important cloth industry. Many towns all over England regarded Winchester's particular and highly-developed forms of local government as a model to be followed in their own endeavours to gain privileges by royal charter.

The Winchester Seal for Debts, Edward I

A complication and a hindrance to Portsmouth's growth was the claim of Southampton to include the town as being within the port of Southampton. Portsmouth's first charter was granted by Richard I in 1194, a grant illustrating that town's connection with Winchester, for the town was given a fair with the same liberties as those 'who attended the fairs at Winchester and Hoyland', and burgesses were to hold their tenants 'as freely as the citizens of Winchester and Oxford hold theirs'. In 1256 Portsmouth obtained the right to have a Gild Merchant, and the town's custumal or code of byelaws, was finally

Medieval Wintonian—graffito

drawn up at the end of the 13th century, a little later than its model, the Winchester Usages.

Amongst the smaller Hampshire towns, Basingstoke had no Merchant Gild but it was an important market centre for the north-west of the county. The impressive ruins of the Chapel of the Gild of the Holy Ghost (once housing the members of an important religious gild, a community whose interests were not only commercial) are a reminder that religious gilds formed an important part of medieval life. Alresford was an episcopal, manorial, town which flourished very largely because of an annual fair granted by John to Bishop Godfrey de Lucy. Romsey was an important road centre, a little town which grew up in the shelter of a great abbey, its development obviously related to the grants of markets made to various Abbesses of Romsey by Henry I, Henry II, and Henry III.

All Hampshire towns were closely united by their conscious knowledge of each others's constitutional development, embodied in royal charters granting privileges based on earlier similar grants to other towns, and by the economic ties of trade and commerce. Though many small towns and villages were virtually self-supporting, iron and salt were two vital commodities which had to be re-distributed. Southampton was the great parent distributing centre of necessities and luxuries alike and the famous fair on St. Giles' Hill at Winchester provided a further opportunity for merchants to meet not only their Hampshire friends, but also traders from France, from Spain, the Low Countries and Italy, who sold wines, silks, strange fruits, pet monkeys and spices. The first sugar ever bought in England was purchased at Winchester in the reign of Henry III.

Every Hampshire town had, and still has, its own special features of topography and layout. Most of medieval Winchester was contained within a walled area pierced by five gates and at least one postern, a wall which probably followed the line of the Roman fortification. An early suburb outside the Westgate declined in importance as the area of the castle encroached on townspeople's houses. There were later suburban developments at Hyde, around the new buildings of Hyde Abbey, and to the south of the city in the area known as the Aldermanry of Kingsgate. Moreover, a vast part of the town outside of the eastern wall was under the jurisdiction of the Bishop of Winchester, and his 'Soke' was a place of refuge to those craftsmen, especially cloth workers, who wished to escape from the tiresome commercial regulations of the Corporation. The maintenance of the walls of Winchester was a fairly continual financial burden levied on the citizens by means of the wall tax or murage. In Southampton the wall was of much later origin and the deficiency of the defences was

46

one of the reasons why the French were able to pillage and sack the town so completely in 1338. Yet poor as the defences were, in Southampton as well as in Winchester, the medieval period, on the whole, was a period of commercial and industrial prosperity. There were many wealthy merchants who could build themselves houses of stone with a first-floor *solar,* amass large fortunes, and give away some of their money to the Church. In the 12th century a Southampton merchant, Gervase de Hampton, lived in his great West Hall, a large house with an upper room with an oriel window, with a series of small buildings around it, surrounded by a high wall, and having its own pleasure garden. In Winchester, Thomas Palmer, alias Moraunt, a wealthy goldsmith had a rather more modest establishment in Calpe Street which was known as 'Moraunt's halle' many years after Moraunt, its builder, had died. Marriage was often a business transaction leading to the accumulation of private fortunes and much real estate. The lady known as Dame Claramund who lived in a large house near St. Michael's church at Southampton and who had two husbands, eventually owned a great many Southampton houses, and when she died in *c.* 1260 left part of her estate to God's House and to the Priory of St. Denys. The many Winchester properties of Hugh de Craan, mayor or the city in 1357, 1365–6 and 1369–70, were partly the result of successful property speculations and partly the result of Craan's marriage with a county heiress, Isabella, the widow of John de Ingepenne.

The Bargate, Southampton

The majority of townsfolk were not wealthy, nor were they even very comfortably housed. Most town houses in Hampshire, not a 'stone' country, were of simple timber-framed construction with roofs of thatching of reeds or straw. In larger houses cooking was often done in a detached, single-storeyed kitchen in the back yard which was an inevitable feature of most town dwellings. Refuse was burnt, or buried in pits, or thrown out into the streets, though there were frequent attempts by the local authorities to prevent the more obvious abuses. Winchester forbade its burgesses to keep pigs in the High Street, its butchers to throw offal in the brooks, and all towns were supposed to enforce the national regulations concerning the quality of ale brewed and bread baked. All industrial processes, and all those people engaged in industry, whether as apprentices, journeymen, or master craftsmen, were subject in theory at least to stringent rules made by the local corporations or by the craft gilds, which eventually succeeded the Merchant Gild. Fines for industrial infringements were used to relieve needy brethren, help widows, or for social functions like the great torchlight procession of the craft gilds of Winchester on the Feast of Corpus Christi. Industry was domestic, carried on in the home, which was often a retail shop as well.

Before the Black Death, the majority of successful Hampshire merchants were probably general dealers, perhaps with large interests in the wholesale supply of wool or of wine, but ready to buy or sell anything in which they could see a useful profit. It was not always easy to know what to do with the large sums which they accumulated. After the expulsion of the Jews in 1290, and even before that date, some Hampshire Christians, the Dalrons, for example, went into the moneylending business. Others bought pieces of silver plate and jewellery to pass down to their heirs; many more made bequests to the many religious houses and no man who made a will ever forgot his own parish church. For the majority of successful Hampshire townspeople it was simple and lucrative to invest in real property, either in the town or in the neighbouring countryside where many citizens bought or leased small country estates. Thus there was movement between town and country and since most Hampshire medieval towns by modern standards were but large villages there was much mutual understanding and sympathy between rustic and townsmen.

12. Medieval shepherds, *c.* 1140: from a psalter of St. Swithun's Priory. (MS B. R. Cotton, Nero c vi)

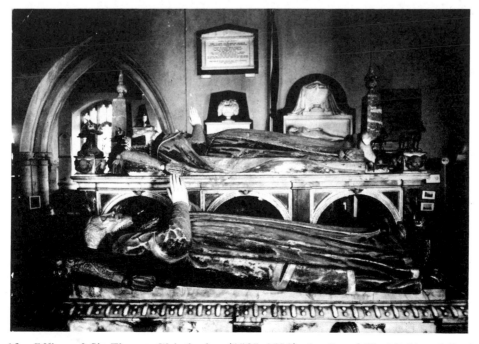

13. Effigy of Sir Thomas Wriothesley (1505–1550), 1st Baron Titchfield and Earl of Southampton; Titchfield Church.

14. Bembridge windmill, Isle of Wight.

VIII The Medieval Countryside

Agriculture has for long been the staple industry of Hampshire and its development, from the time of the Norman Conquest onwards, has been largely determined by the varying physical characteristics of differing parts of the county. A very large area is covered by downland, with much thin, poor chalky soil, land eminently suitable for sheep-grazing. The valleys of the many Hampshire rivers are more fertile and can be very productive when water meadows are properly irrigated. Much of the soil of the New Forest area is poor and gravelly and quite unsuitable for grain-growing. According to William Cobbett some of the best and earliest corn grown in England had long been raised at the foot of Portsdown Hill, but in medieval Hampshire there was little initiative to produce a high-quality agricultural crop of any kind; some of the best products probably came from a kind of model farm run by the Priory of St. Swithun at Silkstead.

Chilcomb church

The method by which medieval Hampshire was farmed can conviently be called the 'manorial system', but it must again be said that there was no real system and no real measure of uniformity; a 'manor' was sometimes a single house, large or small, sometimes a small village or hamlet, sometimes a very large area of land like the manors of Chilcomb, or Crondall. The amount of land in a manor varied considerably. The divisions of the county into 'manors' is convenient, and it is followed by the *Victoria County History,* which describes Hampshire in terms of Hundreds, each Hundred being made up by many manors. Though it is dangerous to generalise, it can be said that the chief characteristics of medieval farming were the very large fields, large and unenclosed, in which every man had a holding the size of which depended on his status in the community. All the land belonged to the manorial overlord, and the lord's own holding, worked on his behalf by his tenants, and for his benefit, was said to be 'in demesne'. There is some evidence that about half of Hampshire retained a primitive two-field system of crop rotation until the 13th century when three open fields became more usual. Open fields were not so frequently found on either side of Southampton Water where there was much marsh and forest land, but even marsh and forest land was often subject to the same proportional use by peasants living near by. The varieties of soil and elevation did not make for uniformity in farming methods, but there is no doubt that much of Hampshire

The Courthouse, East Meon

was not suitable for the primitive arable farming methods of the Middle Ages, and it has been suggested that real arable strip farming was only to be found in very limited areas in the county.

Villages were small and had few permanent buildings, for there was no easily-worked local stone. Considerable use was also made of another traditional and local building material, chalk, which could be easily quarried out of the sides of hills and downs, and was used for walls, for making coffins, and occasionally, as at Selborne Priory, for substantial medieval building. When stone was used, it was nearly always brought via Southampton from Binstead in the Isle of Wight, from Beer in Devon, or from Caen in Normandy. Certain important buildings were roofed in large tiles made of slate from the West Country, and slate also formed an important part of Southampton's coastal trade. Encaustic (decorated) tiles were often used to cover the floors of many churches and monastic buildings, and much use was made of Hampshire's cheapest building material, the flint which could be so easily gathered from fields by cheap and hard labour. Large private houses in the county, whether manors, castles or farms, were usually built of a mixture of stone and flint, but in contrast to great dwellings, the average Hampshire peasant lived in a modest cottage-hut of wattle and daub, with a roof of straw or reed thatch which often caught fire. Amongst larger medieval county houses which survive in part today, much of the walling of the episcopal palace at Bishop's Waltham is of flint; the Courthouse at East Meon (which has windows and a roof which appears to date from the 14th century) has a stone fireplace and a stone-corbelled head said to be a portrait of King John. Some Hampshire manor houses have been the subject of recent archaeological excavations, including Micheldever, Marwell, once a country house of the bishops of Winchester, where the mewes have been identified, and the great house at Wickham, once belonging to Hugh de Port. It has the inevitable moat and a cobbled courtyard dating from a later building of *c.* 1300, when the estate belonged to the de Scures family.

A general survey of Hampshire agriculture in the Middle Ages before the Black Death is not possible, but surviving records do give a clear picture of certain rural communities. At Highclere, in the north of the county, the bishop's manor house has a great mansion with many outbuildings, including granges for wood and logs, a dovecot and a brewery. The house was the *caput,* that is the centre of a large area including Burghclere and Ecchinswell. The farm grew many kinds of crops, barley, oats, peas and vetches, but its chief product was wool from the many sheep grazing in the valley between Beacon Hill and Sidown Range. Italian merchants bought this wool, and Englishmen,

50

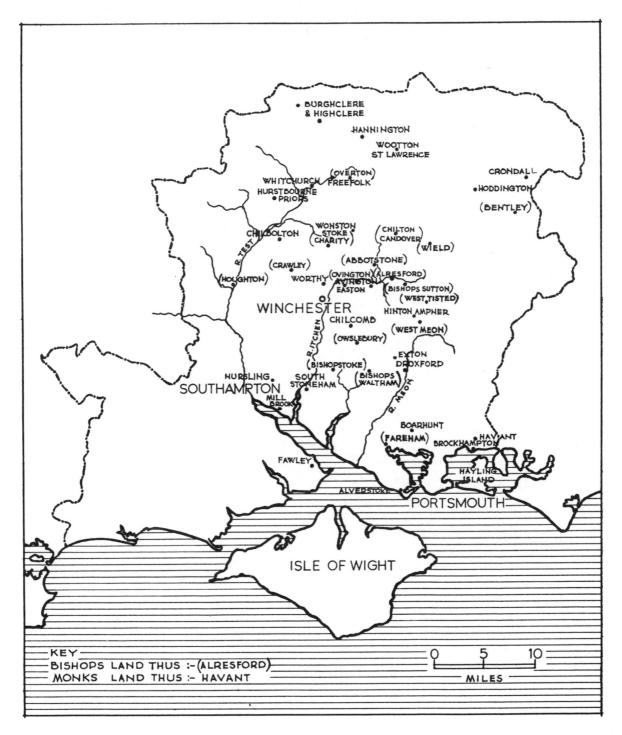

Map 6. Some Estates of the Bishop of Winchester and those of his monks.

51

including the famous Simon the Draper of Winchester. Farther south, at Crawley, there is much to be learnt of how the open field system worked in Hampshire. In both north and south Crawley there were three great open fields, each used for a rotation of crops which seems to have been first fallow when the beasts were turned on to the land, then winter grain followed by spring grain. Most of the hard work of Hampshire farming was done by villeins who had to work the demesne land for their lord as well as look after their own strip-plots. In many areas, the proportion of free tenants to villeins was small. At Compton, an estate belonging to the Priory of St. Swithun, there were only four free tenants in 1287: one of them was the reeve of the village, who paid a rent including a measure of strawberries to be delivered each year to the Infirmary of the Priory. At Morestead the most prominent free tenant was Bernard le Moyne, who had to provide the Priory with 550 eggs at Christmas and two-thirds of a bushel of strawberries on St. John's Day. His holding can be identified with the present Old Down Farm. At Silkstead the Priory kept a model farm served by a permanent resident staff, and here the priors often spent a summer holiday. Grapes were grown regularly in the vineyards at Silkstead, peafowl bred for the table, and a great pigeon house built in 1307 provided a welcome addition to plain winter fare.

Just as the manors varied in acreage, so, too, the holdings held by individual tenants differed enormously in size and in productivity. In the village of Yateley, a number of Priory tenants held virgates of land but the virgate varied in size from 12½ acres upwards; all over Hampshire holdings passed from father to son, or from a tenant to his widow simply by the immemorial custom of each manor, declared in the manor court, and made valid by the payment of fine (a fee usually paid in goods or services) to the lord. Manorial lords thus had several sources of revenue, and potential capital resources, rents, profits from sale of surplus product, and the fines of their courts.

The life of every village was regulated by the custom of the manor to which it belonged, and this regulation was carried out by the manorial court which met regularly, to punish infringements of the custom, and to accept new tenants for vacant holdings, a profitable procedure since every new holder of land had to pay his lord a heriot, a fine to succeed as heir, usually his best animal, or its equivalent in money. All the normal farming processes necessary to work the land were divided out amongst the lord's unfree tenants, according to the custom of the manor. The most important surviving group of these customs is contained in the custumal of St. Swithun's Priory, written down to the end of the 13th century and providing much information about the customs of the Priory manors all over Hampshire. Men and women were required to work the lord's land at harvest time, or to send a substitute, to plough, to carry the seed from the lord's court to where it had to be sown, to help with threshing, and with the making of manure heaps. Unfree tenants, like Walter de la Lane at Swansdrop in Crondall, could neither sell a house nor an ox, nor marry off their daughters without payment of fine to the lord. At Yateley, near by, a comparatively large holding of over 100 acres, held by Juliana de Aula, was rented by a wide variety of payments in money and in kind, four stoups of honey, two hens at Christmas, and 20 eggs at Easter, as well as services of ploughing, reaping and weeding the lord's land. Commutation, the substitution of money rents for services, only came in very slowly towards the end of the 13th century, and Hampshire villages were largely self-supporting, and the only essentials which had to be brought from a distance were salt and iron. There was little market gardening of fruit or vegetables for re-sale, and the chief and essential aim of medieval farming was the production of a food and drink grain crop to provide bread and beer for the farming community itself and for the manorial overlord, though obviously some supplies were grown deliberately for certain market towns. Stock raising was very hazardous indeed, animals were small, frequently ravaged by disease, and there was no incentive to careful or selective breeding, for most animals were grazed or pastured together on open or common land. The many references to fencing or enclosure often prove to be temporary arrangements, made for example at lambing time. For the average Hampshire peasant life was often harsh, short, and wearing, an existence only lightened by the holy days of the church.

Deer—medieval graffito

One of the most interesting of all controversies affecting the economy of the medieval countryside concerns the New Forest. It used to be said that the making of the Forest was William the Conqueror's great Hampshire crime. Yet even the most detailed study of Domesday Book fails to produce evidence other than the indubitable fact that a number of holdings had been taken into the Forest by 1086 either completely or in part. There is no evidence at all from any source to suggest that the Conqueror obliterated vast numbers of towns and villages or demolished 60 churches. Much of the area has very poor soil, and it could never have sustained a large population. In prehistoric times the Forest afforded shelter, but there are only slight traces of early habitation—Beaker folk at Fordingbridge, Minstead, Lymington, and Hurn; the population may have increased in the late Bronze Age, for a number of cemeteries survive from this period, and Bronze Age man and his successors all used Hengistbury Head with its many natural advantages as a Hampshire landing-place. In the Roman period the timber and brushwood of the New Forest was used in the widely scattered kilns making greyish and red and white pottery. Even in 1100 the Forest was called Ytene, land of the Jutes, and it was probably these people whose descendants were working the few acres of good land and making a few clearings in the later Anglo-Saxon period. Forest place-names ending in -ley, -wood, and -hurst, and -shaw, are indications of this kind of change. Cnut fined those who hunted his Forest illegally, but in the early medieval period Forest law was much more severe; death and mutilation were the penalties, and the royal hunter's course was unimpeded, for until 1483 it was illegal to make any kind of enclosure for the protection of young trees or of animals. Some of the inhabitants, however, did benefit by 'Commoner's Rights', the privilege of turning out livestock to graze in the Forest at certain periods. Instead of the normal kind of manorial court found in other parts of Hampshire, Courts of Regard, Attachment and Swainmote dealt with human and with canine offenders against Forest Laws, and special Justices visited the area regularly to punish the most serious infringements.

Stone was even more infrequently used for building in the New Forest than it was in other parts of Hampshire countryside. A mixture of heather and clay produced walls of 'cob', the usual material of domestic buildings, stone being reserved for churches, and for the great Cistercian abbey of Beaulieu, the Forest's most important medieval building.

IX Hampshire During the Black Death and the 100 Years' War (1337-1444)

The great dynastic struggle between the rival houses of France and England which began in 1337, lasted for more than the 100 years which gave it its name. It was a period of great change in Hampshire, of social unrest, of major economic trouble, and problems of decline in population. The county was vulnerable to attacks from France and her allies, and the wool trade suffered from the vicissitudes of war. Men were called away from the land, and before long the Black Death seriously upset the economy of a county unused to rapid social change. The Black Death may have resulted in a violent break up of the manorial system, but it has also been suggested that it was merely part of the pattern of what can be called normal medieval catastrophe, of recurring plague on mankind, murrain on sheep, famine, and the devastations of war. Recent research has shown that the population of the county had begun to decline before Hampshire suffered in the great European famine of 1315-17, and Hampshire farms lying on the route of men marching to war were always dangerously situated. The reeve at Silkstead paid fairly large and regular sums in bribes to prevent his stock being harmed or his corn carts taken for military transport.

In October 1348 the Bishop of Winchester, Edington, who had already received news of the Black Death and of its dreadful effects on the Continent, issued special directions for prayers and processions for the monks of his Cathedral Church for he was 'struck with the great fear lest, which God forbid, the foul disease ravage any part of our city and diocese'. The plague was already in Dorset, and by the turn of the winter of 1348 and 1349, it was at its height in Hampshire. Though this initial outbreak diminished by the end of 1349, there were further severe outbreaks in 1361-2, 1369, and 1379. All the available evidence suggests that the plague of 1348-9 shook the agrarian economy of much of Hampshire and it certainly devastated Winchester. Amongst the farms belonging to Titchfield Abbey there was a high mortality on the coast, at Titchfield itself in particular, but a high death rate is also indicated in certain inland areas, in Burghclere and Highclere; for example, as late as 1376 at Highclere, of 103 ploughing services due only 15 were actually performed, and in Burghclere the proportion was 207 to 54. In central Hampshire, the earliest record surviving for Silkstead after the first outbreaks of plague shows a considerable diminution in the numbers of cattle, sheep and pigs, and

Titchfield Abbey Seal

55

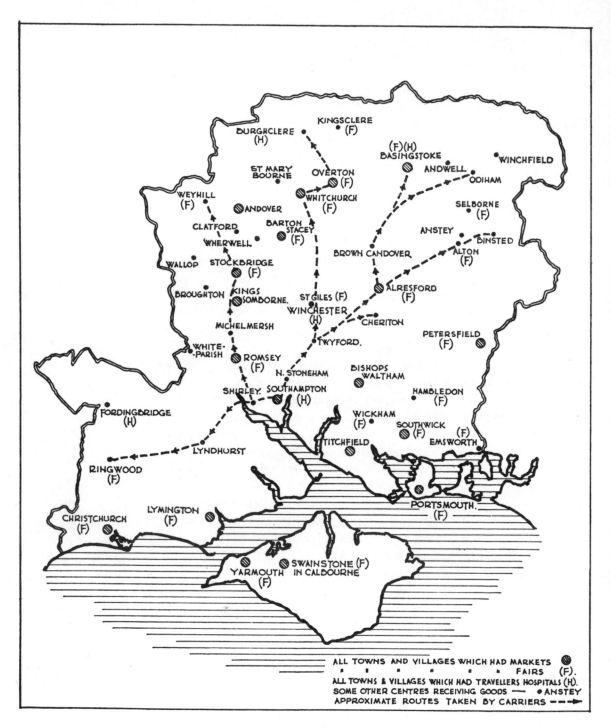

Map 7. Internal trade in late medieval Hampshire.

56

15a. The Vyne, near Basingstoke.

15b. Bournemouth pier.

16.   Palace House, Beaulieu.

17.   Stanbridge Earls: built by George Gollop in 1653, on an old site.

18. Christopher Saxton's map of Hampshire, drawn 1575.

Hamshire.	Winchester.	Portesmouth.	Fareham.	Hauant.	Petersfield.	Alton.	Alresforde.	B. Waltham.	Kingesclere.	Andouer.	Rumsey.	Fording-bridge.	Ringwood.	Christ-Church.	S. Hampton.	Basingstoke.	Ouerton.	Wickham.	Titchefield.	Beaulieu.	Lymington.	Odiam.	Micheldouer.	Whit-Church.	Stoke-bridge.	Hertford-bridge.
Bramfhot.	18	23	20	16	8	6	12	17	20	24	25	37	38	43	25	13	18	18	22	32	35	10	16	20	24	12
Hertford bridge.	24	32	29	28	17	9	17	24	14	24	30	40	44	48	32	8	16	27	30	38	4	5	18	18	27	
Stoke-bridge.	6	23	18	23	20	20	8	13	16	16	7	15	19	25	13	18	12	15	18	17	20	22	9	10		
Whit-church.	11	28	23	26	18	22	11	16	6	16	24	30	38	21	9	3	20	23	26	30	14	6				
Micheldouer.	9	22	18	21	12	11	6	12	10	8	13	23	27	32	17	9	6	15	18	23	25	13				
Odyam.	19	28	24	24	14	5	12	20	11	19	25	36	38	44	24	4	11	23	26	34	37					
Lymington.	18	16	15	20	26	32	24	20	35	25	13	11	3	9	9	34	30	16	13	4						
Beaulieu.	16	14	12	17	30	28	20	12	32	22	11	12	11	13	5	32	27	12	10							
Titchefield.	12	7	2	9	14	21	14	6	27	21	11	19	20	21	6	25	26	3								
Wickham.	10	8	3	8	11	18	11	20	24	20	11	20	21	24	8	22	20									
Ouerton.	12	27	22	26	17	12	10	16	5	8	17	26	30	36	22	7										
Bafingftoke.	16	28	24	25	15	7	11	18	6	16	22	32	36	41	25											
S. Hampton.	10	12	8	14	17	23	15	8	26	19	7	13	14	17												
Chrift-Church.	26	26	24	29	35	40	32	24	41	30	20	11	6													
Ryngwood.	20	23	22	28	29	6	27	22	36	24	14	5														
Fording-Bridge.	17	24	21	28	29	32	24	19	31	20	11															
Rumfey.	7	18	13	20	19	22	13	10	22	12																
Andouer.	10	27	20	27	20	18	13	16	11																	
Kingefclere.	16	32	26	29	20	13	13	21																		
B. Waltham.	6	11	6	11	10	15	8																			
Alresforde.	7	18	14	16	8	8																				
Alton.	15	23	20	19	8																					
Petersfeild.	13	15	12	11																						
Hauant.	17	8	7																							
Fareham.	13	5																								
Portefmouth.	22																									

The vfe of this Table.

THe Townes or places betweene which you defire to know, the diftance you may finde in the names of the Townes in the vpper part and in the fide, and bring them in a fquare as the lines will guide you : and in the fquare you fhall finde the figures which declare the diftance of the miles.

And if you finde any place in the fide which will not extend to make afquare with that aboue, then feeking that aboue which will not extend to make a fquare, and fee that in the vpper, and the other fide, and it will fhowe you the diftance. It is familiar and eafie.

Beare with defectes, the vfe is neceffarie.

Inuented by IOHN NORDEN.

19. (*left*) 'The Table for Hampshire', from John Norden's *England: an Intended Guide for English Travailers*, 1625.

20a. Andover High Street and market.

20b. Broad Street, Alresford.

fewer people to look after the stock; there were vacant buildings at Compton which were not let again fully for as long as 20 years after 1349, 15 families died out completely, and by 1352 the most important freeman had to mortgage his property to a London merchant. Some villages were practically wiped out, especially if they suffered in a later outbreak; thus by 1362, most of the Morestead village houses were in ruins. Manorial lords found it often difficult to find tenants, though this was not the case with many of the Titchfield holdings, which were at least nominally filled, though sometimes apparently by mere children. The Isle of Wight is said to have been virtually depopulated; Brading sea mill was vacant in 1349 for 'no Miller would come because of the mortality'; the average number of *Inquisitiones port mortem,* in the Island (inquiries after death concerning the property of notable persons) was one a year, but in 1349 there were seven deaths thus recorded, all people of considerable local importance. There is no doubt, either, that there was a very high death rate amongst the clergy all over the county; the high mortality is referred to in Bishop Edington's register in an entry of 14 January 1348-9, and for that year, out of a total of some 83 livings vacant, 30 at least were caused by death. Amongst those who died there were the incumbents of Farnham, Wallop, Hurstbourne, Abbott's Ann, Greatham, South Tidworth, Crondall, Amport, and Basingstoke, as well as the Prior of Christchurch and St. Swithun's and the Abbess of St. Mary's, Winchester. In the first three months of 1349 there were at least six vacant livings caused by death in the city of Winchester and many churches fell into disuse, amongst them St. Lawrence in the very heart of Winchester, where the rector was allowed to find another living because of the ruin of his parish. It was necessary for Bishop William of Wykeham to threaten to excommunicate laymen who dismantled churches or usurped their sites, and in 1376 the mayor and bailiffs of Winchester were actually cited to appear in the cathedral before the bishop for illegally taking the sites of St. Petroc, St. Martin in the Wall, and St. Nicholas. Many years after, Winchester was said to be in such a state of economic decline that there were in 1452 nearly 1,000 houses empty or in ruins, and 17 parish churches inofficiate. The decline was definite, but it was only in part a result of the Black Death, other factors being the difficulties of the woollen cloth industry, and the restrictive regulations of the Corporation which drove men to live anywhere rather than within the walls of Winchester, regulations which in fact helped to produce a revolt in 1381 against the city's burgher oligarchy.

The centre of Winchester before 1348 was tightly packed and disease spread rapidly. Even though the town had the advantage of many streams and brooks running through it and two large public lavatories, the only conduited water supply was for the monks of the cathedral, and the townspeople took their water from the brooks and from wells, including the common city well near the High Cross. From the early years of Edward I's reign, in contrast, the townspeople of Southampton had a good water supply, thanks to the grant to the town of a conduit house and piped water supply by the Friars Minor. Perhaps on the whole Southampton was healthier and less cramped than Winchester, but in 1338 the town was sacked by the French and much of it had to be rebuilt. Though the townspeople had been given numerous murage grants to complete the walling, in fact the work had not been carried out. It was feared that the French might return, trade suffered and some merchants moved to Bristol. The Black Death was a further blow and by the last quarter of the 14th century, the population of Southampton has been calculated as less than two thousand. A period of security and revived trade followed the temporary peace with France in 1389, and the presence of many Italian merchants was a very important factor in the prosperity of late medieval Southampton, when colonies of Venetian and Genoese traders and other Italian merchants from Florence and Milan helped to make the town a cosmopolitan centre. The greater part of Southampton's varied imports was distributed through Bargate by carriers to many parts of southern England. In the reign of Henry V the king's attempts to create a Royal Navy were centred on Southampton, for it was a Southampton draper and general contractor, William Soper, whose father had been a Winchester merchant, who constructed several of Henry's most important ships, including the *Grace Dieu,* the largest ship to be built in England before 1637. War thus brought a temporary prosperity to Southampton, but Henry VI's advisers sold most of the Royal Navy by auction in 1422, and Southampton was never again a likely centre for naval development.

Thus the years of the Hundred Years' War were years of difficulty and decline for Hampshire towns, though decline was sometimes temporarily camouflaged by the false prosperity brought about by the bustle of war and the individual fortunes made by contractors like Soper in Southampton, and by innkeepers such as Mark le Faire in Winchester. In the county generally there was recovery, but a definite decline in population, and the process of change by which money rents were paid instead of services given, was accentuated. More and more demesne land was farmed out for a paid rent by lords who could not otherwise get their land worked at all; on some manors the large common fields decreased in size and some were eventually cut up. Yet it was not mere economic and social change which was to prove the most important sign of the end of the Middle Ages. The brutalities of war, and the horrors of the Black Death, shook men's faith and belief in the teaching of the Church. It was not always easy to believe in the resurrection of the body or the sacredness of human life; the rebuilding of much of Winchester Cathedral begun by Bishop Edington and completed by William of Wykeham stands as a great act of faith in a world of increasing religious difficulties and of declining moral values.

Bishop William of Wykeham

X The Diocese of Winchester Before the Reformation

Christchurch Priory, misericord

Seal of Selborne Priory

Religious life in medieval Hampshire owed much to the dedicated men and women whose lives were spent within the walls of monasteries and convents. After the Norman Conquest, the number of monastic houses increased and to the older Benedictine communities of nuns at St. Mary's, Winchester, Wherwell and Romsey, of monks at Newminster and Old Minster in Winchester, were added Cistercian monasteries at Quarr (Isle of Wight) (*c.* 1132), Beaulieu (1204), and Netley (1239), a small Cistercian nunnery at Wintney (before 1200), as well as other quasi-monastic establishments of canons following the Rule of St. Augustine. The Cistercians, whose order was named from the parent house of Citeaux in Burgundy and whose greatest member in medieval Christendom was St. Bernard of Clairvaux, were fundamentally not a new order of monks, but a severe and rigidly reformed community following the Benedictine rule with simplicity on secluded sites away from worldly distractions. Manual labour was an important part of their daily life and each house had its own *conversi*, lay brethren who were not likely to become monks but were a second order occupied in much hard manual work. There were thus many opportunities within each Cistercian house for men and women who were not of the intellectual standard associated with Benedictine monasteries. Unlike the Benedictines, however, Cistercian foundations were not great feudal landowners, and their income was largely derived from their own physical efforts. Sheep-farming and forestry were the chief occupations of the monks of Netley and Beaulieu. Both Cistercians and Benedictine monks were 'regulars', that is real monks following a definite 'rule', *regula*. Another kind of ecclesiastical foundation was that provided by the houses of canons, secular priests following the so-called rule of St. Augustine, who lived a communal life in their houses at Breamore (founded *c.* 1128–33), Portchester (1133), which later moved to Southwick (1145–53), St. Denys, Southampton (1127), Christchurch (*c.* 1150), Mottisfont (1201), and Selborne (1233). An additional house of canons of the order of Prémontre was founded at Titchfield in *c.* 1232, whose inhabitants, 'white' canons, to distinguish them from the 'black' canons of the order of St. Augustine, did much the same sort of religious work, preaching as missionaries, acting as parish priests, and devoting a large part of their time, at least in the early years of their houses, to manual labour on their estates.

Of other religious houses, only the Benedictines were subject to episcopal control by visitations and subsequent injunctions, and medieval bishops often found it necessary to inquire into, control and reform the houses under their care. Bishops of Winchester have always had a particular relationship with the cathedral Benedictine priory, being elected by the Prior and his monks (later the Dean and Chapter); a tradition which in theory remains unbroken today. Once elected, the relationship between the monks and the bishop was almost that of a monastery with its abbot, and the cathedral fabric is almost entirely the work of a series of changes instituted and paid for by successive diocesan bishops.

Arms of the diocese of Winchester

The first Norman bishop, a friend of William Rufus, Walkelin (1070–98) rebuilt the cathedral entirely and pulled down the Old Minster. He also seems to have built himself a palace at East Meon. William Giffard (1107–29) was the first of many Winchester bishops to be also Chancellors of England, and was one of the earliest of the English bishops to recognise the Cistercian revival of monasticism, by the foundation just over the Hampshire border (but in the diocese) of Waverley Abbey in 1128. His successor, Henry de Blois, (1128–71), was an outstanding bishop in every way. A Cluniac monk, and brother of that Stephen who was one of the claimants to the English throne after the death of Henry I in 1135, his early career was that of a politician and scholar rather than that of an ecclesiastic. As well as being Bishop of Winchester he was also Abbot of Glastonbury, which he re-adorned and enriched with great generosity from a vast private fortune. This fortune also enabled him to give munificently to Winchester Cathedral and to found the most famous almshouse in the kingdom, the Hospital of the Holy Cross at Sparkford, better known as St. Cross. His ambitions were unbounded; he was actually elected Archbishop of Canterbury in 1136 and when his enemies in Rome prevented the Pope from confirming the election, de Blois got himself made Papal Legate in England, with precedence over the Archbishop of Canterbury. Later on, he tried—but in vain—to have Winchester made into an archbishopric and in the south-eastern corner of the city built a great episcopal palace, Wolvesey. He constructed other great fortified castle residences at Merdon, Farnham and Bishop's Waltham, valuable military strongholds for a bishop actively engaged in civil war. At the accession of Henry II in 1154, de Blois went into exile, back to his old monastery at Cluny, whence he returned about about three years later, a reformed character, a benevolent elder statesman, and the senior English bishop. Though as Chancellor, Thomas Becket had helped to demolish de Blois's castles, the Bishop supported Thomas as Archbishop in his struggle

Henry de Blois

61

Hyde Abbey
Romanesque Capital

A second
Hyde Capital

with Henry II, and he died in 1171, a venerable and beloved statesman. De Blois's episcopate is contemporary with that great artistic revival known as the Romanesque renaissance of the 12th century, a revival exemplified by a severe and dignified architectural style, by carving in ivory, by sumptuous metal and enamel work, by richly-embossed bookbinding, and by a style of manuscript illumination which reached its greatest beauty and power in the Latin Vulgate known as the Winchester Bible.

The revenues of the medieval bishopric were in fact so large that it was difficult for medieval bishops of Winchester not to be generous. A large proportion of the bishop's income came from his many and scattered Hampshire estates; some of this income was in money, a proportion was in goods in kind, either used directly by the bishop and his household when he stayed in the district, or sent by local officials whenever required. All the many local officials kept detailed accounts compiled eventually into a great series of records known as the Bishop of Winchester's Pipe Rolls, a wonderful series, beginning in 1208, which provide a detailed and complete account of the manorial estates of the Bishops of Winchester. The records were kept as rolls till 1454; after that date they continue as folios and though not every manor is mentioned individually every time, the general picture is complete and provides a fascinating story of a great feudal itinerant household with a central treasury under a steward or seneschal at Wolvesey, Winchester. Some bishops had the help of a suffragan or of an assistant bishop and indeed this was apparently quite usual in the 14th century. Suffragans were usually bishops *'in partibus'*, that is to say bishops with foreign titles, for example Peter Corbaviensis (1322-31), William Salubiensis (1407-1417), or they were Irish diocesan bishops acting in England; one suffragan, Caesarius de Rosis (1349-55) is said to have been a Franciscan. Much of the routine work of the diocese was carried out by the Archdeacons of Surrey and of Winchester. The usual form of address for an archdeacon was simply Dominus, and the use of 'Venerable' did not apparently appear persistently in the Winchester diocese until after 1802. It was the archdeacon's duty, on receipt of a mandate from the bishop, to induct the clerics appointed to vacate livings, and sometimes he carried out the induction in person and sometimes by deputy. Another essential part of diocesan organisation was the procedure for proving wills, which had to be proved before officials of the bishop or of the archdeacons, unless they were made by people living in a limited number of districts called 'Peculiars', having their own procedure. Disputes about legacies or wills were dealt with by the Bishop's Consistory Court which was held in any suitable church in the early medieval period,

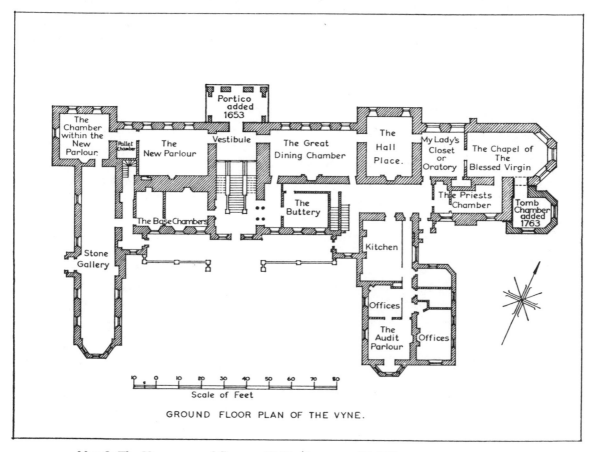

The Chamber within the New Parlour

Pallet Chamber

The New Parlour

Vestibule

Portico added 1653

The Great Dining Chamber

The Hall Place.

My Lady's Closet or Oratory

The Chapel of The Blessed Virgin

The Base Chambers

The Buttery

The Priests Chamber

Tomb Chamber added 1763

Stone Gallery

Kitchen

Offices

The Audit Parlour

Offices

10 5 0 10 20 30 40 50 60 70 80
Scale of Feet

GROUND FLOOR PLAN OF THE VYNE.

Map 8. The Vyne, ground floor, c. 1540. (See pages 70–71)

but from about 1404 was housed in a special gallery built at the west
end of the north aisle of Winchester Cathedral. The Consistory Court
also dealt with matrimonial disputes, and cases which concerned the
discipline of the clergy. All the various official acts of each bishop,
important documents of his episcopate, visitations, notes of ordinations
and inductions, were kept, and still are kept by each bishop's Registrar
in a volume therefore called the Register.

The medieval diocese of Winchester was very large, and the bishops
moved round it slowly in comfort and dignity when they were not
engaged elsewhere as royal civil servants or politicians. It included
the counties of Hampshire and of Surrey, and also the present dioceses
of Portsmouth and Guildford, but not the Channel Islands, which only
came into the care of the Bishop of Winchester in the 16th century.
In London, the bishop had a large palatial home, Winchester House
at Southwark, as well as a prison known as the Clink, and within the
diocese he had many residences.

The Bishop's Palace, Bishops Waltham

In 1208 Bishop Peter de Roches, like all his medieval successors, had three chief seats, at Farnham, Winchester, and Taunton, Somerset, and secondary residences at Waltham, Clere, Downton and Merdon, Marwell, and Bishop's Waltham. His manors at Fareham and at Bitterne (on the site of the Roman port of *Clausentum*) were centres for the essential redistribution of wine and salt. Though the accounts give much information about the economic aspects of the Bishop's political activities, they also show de Roches as the purchaser of hawks and hunting dogs, for like his king, John, the bishop was a keen huntsman. Every bishop had a large personal retinue of clerics and of laymen, many of whom attended on him because of the work he did in his other capacities.

It is almost surprising, in fact, to find that most medieval bishops did devote so much time to the ecclesiastical duties of their diocese. Bishop John de Pontoise (or Pontissara, 1282–1304), founded a great chapel at Winchester, served by a College of secular priests, and dedicated to St. Elizabeth of Hungary, where masses were to be said daily for the souls of the Bishops of Winchester and of all the faithful. Though there were many parish churches, he seems to have begun the licensing of private chapels in manor houses, amongst them one at Tichborne for the family who were famous as the distributors of a 'dole' of flour given annually to all their village tenants, a custom which still continues. It was during Pontissara's episcopate that a great financial survey was made of the diocese by order of Pope Nicholas IV in order to provide money for the Church. This *Taxatio* shows that most parishes in Hampshire were served by priests who were rectors, though they might not be resident: there were comparatively few vicarages, and these only in benefices with large financial endowments. Yet many of the rectories were small and ill-endowed, and the life of the average parish priest was far removed from the wealth and luxury of the diocesan bishop. Even Bishop John de Pontissara, however, had to borrow money to meet his expenditure when on royal business at Rome. It would be pleasant to think that when he did visit his diocese he rode on the very expensive black palfrey given him by Edward I, just as Henry Woodlock, his successor (1305–1316) rode through the diocese on his palfreys, Braybrook and Bereford. Woodlock loved his work, and unlike most of the Bishops of Winchester, was a Hampshire man and the only Prior of St. Swithun's to become bishop. He was not a politician, and a glance at his itinerary for only one year, 1308, will show how he spent his time in the service of his diocese. Early in 1308 he helped to crown Edward II at Westminster, and then held an ordination at St. Mary Overy, now Southwark Cathedral. In June and July he was at Marwell, Bitterne and East Meon, and on

The Weeke paten

Trinity Sunday ordained 120 candidates at Southampton. By September he was at Highclere and then at Farnham for another big ordination service. In the winter he was again in the Surrey half of the diocese, at Farnham, Esher and Southwark, but spent Christmas at Highclere. A charming letter of invitation to the Prior of St. Swithun's to keep the Christmas of 1310 with him at Wolvesey records Woodlock as friendly and firm; the Prior was definitely to come to Wolvesey, no plea of other engagement to stand in the way.

The Spitting Jew, 15th-century roof boss, Winchester Cathedral

His successor, John Sandale (1316-1319) took some action against pluralists, incumbents who held more than one living, and also against clergy who were non-resident. By visitations and injunctions he rebuked monks and nuns for breaking their rules. A young chaplain, from St. Mary's nunnery, Winchester, strutting round Winchester in a gay parti-coloured habit, had the misfortune to meet the bishop in person. He was severely rebuked, as was the abbess for allowing such a scandal.

The episcopate of William of Edington (1346-1366) was marred by the Black Death, yet Edington's most remembered achievement is that he began the rebuilding of Winchester Cathedral, a task which he did not live to complete. The relations between the diocesan bishops and the Priory Church of St. Swithun in Winchester, their cathedral, has always been of great importance and the cathedral fabric, as it stands today, is almost entirely the work of the bishops of the diocese. The last of the great builders, before the Reformation, were William of Wykeham (1367-1404) and Richard Fox (1501-1528).

Both Wykeham and Fox were remarkable for the energy and time they devoted to the pressing problems of diocesan reform. Wykeham's famous foundation, St. Mary College of Winchester, was founded in 1382 and was designed for 70 poor scholars, its object being to provide a sound education for men who were likely to go into the church. Repeated injunctions in his register reflect the low standard of clerical learning; thus, in 1385, he ordered the rector of St. Michael's in Jewry Street, Winchester, to learn by heart the Creed, the Ten Commandments, and 'other things which a Minister ought to know': an injunction which indicates a lack of elementary standards for a cleric in a cathedral city. There were, however, far too many churches in medieval Winchester for their respective parishes to survive the depletion of the city at the time of the Black Death. Bishop Fox greatly reduced the number by uniting certain livings, and long before his time the problem of church work in the poorer districts and outskirts of Winchester was partly solved by the coming of the Friars, and the erection of four great friary churches. Until the Black Death there was probably never less than 60 active parish churches in Winchester, a great contrast with Portsmouth and Southampton.

XI *The Reformation in Hampshire*

Bishop Fox

During the greater part of the 16th century the minds of Hampshire men and women were troubled and perplexed by the many religious changes of the times, changes of the Reformation and Counter-Reformation, which eventually led to the establishment of a national Anglican Church with the Sovereign at its head, a Church claiming to be Catholic in doctrine but independent of papal authority. The monasteries were the last possible bastion of papal supremacy in England and for this reason, as well as for other political and financial motives, Henry VIII decided to close them.

In some ways, it is the dissolution of the Hampshire monasteries which marks the end of the Middle Ages in Hampshire. Yet it would be a mistake to think that 'Reform' only began in the reign of Henry VIII. Many of the later medieval bishops had shown a keen and informed interest in diocesan affairs. Wykeham's attempts to provide for the education of his clergy led him to found, not a monastery, but two colleges, one at Winchester for boys, the other at New College for undergraduates. The problems of small or inefficient monasteries were noticed long before 1536, and there was a plan to close Mottisfont as early as 1494 which was not proceeded with, though Bishop Waynflete (1447-86) did close Selborne Priory, and used its endowments for his new collegiate foundation of Magdalen College, Oxford. Fox's episcopate (1501-28) was marked by careful and moderate reform, for he instituted the now familiar policy of unifying small benefices in towns, closing redundant churches, and he also completed the work of Edington and Wykeham in the cathedral by improving the choir and giving it a beautiful new wooden vault decorated with carved and coloured bosses. His sympathy towards the new learning of the Renaissance was shown by his foundation of Corpus Christi College, Oxford, and it is significant that he, Wykeham and Waynflete all founded colleges at Oxford, not monasteries in their own diocese. Fox died in 1528, and was succeeded by Cardinal Wolsey, whose tenure of the bishopric was very brief, for he was enthroned by proxy, never held any ordinations and died in 1530. Ecclesiastical appointments made at this time suggest a definite policy of promoting those who were supporters of the government. John Salcot, made Abbot of Hyde, surrendered his abbey at the Dissolution in return for higher office. Anne Boleyn's uncle, William Boleyn, was made Archdeacon of Winchester in January 1530.

ESTATES OF THOMAS WRIOTHESLEY
1ST EARL OF SOUTHAMPTON. THUS :- WARBLINGTON.

ESTATES OF WILLIAM PAULET.
1ST MARQUESS OF WINCHESTER THUS :- (KINGSCLERE.)

FORMER MONASTIC PROPERTY
        UNDERLINED THUS :- BEAULIEU (WRIOTHESLEY)
                  :- (NETLEY)(PAULET)

INHERITED ESTATES OF
        WILLIAM PAULET THUS :- (BASING)

Map 9.   New landlords after the Reformation (in Hampshire).

Titchfield Abbey

The main story of the first half of the Reformation in Hampshire coincides with the episcopate of Bishop Stephen Gardiner, a long period, 1531 to 1555, broken by Gardiner's suspension and imprisonment by the extreme Protestant government of Edward VI, when the bishopric was held by a Protestant reformer, John Poynet. During Poynet's episcopate an arrangement was made with the Crown by which the bishop received a fixed annual revenue in return for the surrender of his lands, but this plan, by which not only the Crown but also the Marquess of Winchester appears to have benefited, was apparently cancelled in the reign of Mary, and the bishops kept their estates till the middle of the 19th century. Yet there is little in the registers of either Gardiner and Poynet to suggest that this was a time when men were giving their lives for their religious beliefs, and nothing at all to show the doctrinal changes or the reactions of Hampshire men to them. The dissolution of the Hampshire monasteries is hardly apparent at all in Gardiner's Register, but a detailed account of the houses was, however, compiled in 1501 by Dr. Thomas Hede when he conducted a visitation of the monasteries at a time when both the sees of Winchester and of Canterbury were vacant.

Hede began his inspection at St. Swithun, Winchester. He found only 35 monks, but nothing to complain of there, or in the other Winchester houses of St. Mary's and Hyde. All the other Hampshire houses were satisfactory, with the exception of St. Denys, Southampton, where one piece of church plate was in pawn, and Romsey where convent life had obviously become almost a farce. A little later on, in 1533, Wherwell Abbey became notorious for a brief while because of the behaviour of its abbess, Anne Colt, but this was an exceptional case; the previous abbess, Alice Cowdreye was said to have been 'pleasant to God and true to the king'. Yet in 1536 no excuse of good conduct or proper administration could save the Hampshire monasteries from the king's determination to close them, and by the end of the year St. Denys, Netley and Quarr had all 'surrendered'. In 1537 Titchfield was closed, and handed over to Thomas Wriothesley who converted the fabric of the church into a great private house. Beaulieu fell to his lot also in 1538, as did Southwick, which eventually passed to one of his servants, John White. At Hyde, Winchester, Wriothesley used the monastery as a stone quarry for his new house at Titchfield, and the complaisant abbot was made Bishop of Salisbury. At St. Swithun's, Winchester, Wriothesley, accompanied by his fellow commissioners Pollard and Williams, and by the mayor or Winchester, and some of the Corporation's 'best brethren' destroyed the great shrine of the patron saint in the middle of the night of September, 1538, for fear of the citizens' disapproval. Yet the cathedral survived, the capitular

Arms of Dean and Chapter of Winchester

body was reformed as a Dean and Chapter, and the last prior, William Kingsmill, became the first dean. At St. Mary's, Winchester, the last abbess, Elizabeth Shelley, surrendered her abbey, retired on a pension, as did the majority of monks and nuns, and continued to live a quasi-conventual life in Winchester with a group of nuns from the abbey.

Sir John Mason, the only Lay Dean of Winchester

Sweeping as these changes were, much of the old doctrine of the Catholic Church remained as before, and it was not until the reign of Edward VI that the real effect of reform was felt. A new liturgy, in English, contained in two successive prayer books superseded the old Latin missal, and liturgical books were thrown away, sold as scrap, or used as covers for the new church parish registers of baptisms, burials and marriages which Thomas Cromwell had ordered every incumbent to keep from 1538 onwards. To quote only a few examples, at St. Michael's, Southampton, and at Southwick, the earliest parish registers are bound in parts of 15th-century missals; at Greatham, a late-medieval Gradual serves as cover; and there are fragments of pre-Reformation theological bindings similarly used on registers at Brockenhurst and Micheldever. In 1550 the churchwardens of St. John, Winchester, sold a hundredweight of old parchment books for six shillings, pieces of alabaster for one shilling and fourpence, and a 'guilded image' for only a shilling, though in 1551–54 they sold a cross and a chalice for the very large sum of £22 17s. 10d. At the beginning of Mary's reign, Bishop Gardiner was released from the Tower, and it was he who officiated at Mary's wedding to Philip of Spain in Winchester Cathedral. The reaction against extreme Protestantism is shown in his resumed register, which records that a number of Hampshire clerics were deprived of their livings, clearly men who had married or those who had accepted the Protestant prayer books.

The dissolution of the monasteries was inevitably followed by the appearance of a new class of landlord in Hampshire. Not all these 'new' men were Protestant reformers: those who kept the old faith included William Laurens of Winchester, a lawyer, who paid for the restoration of the High Cross on the occasion of the marriage of Philip and Mary in Winchester Cathedral, but who had negotiated the royal charter giving the corporation the Winchester rents of some of the dissolved monasteries, a service for which he was rewarded by favourable leases of city property. Other new landlords profited on a much larger scale; Thomas Wriothesley (d. 1550), who became Earl of Southampton, has already been mentioned and perhaps profited more from the Reformation than any other man. In Southampton itself the Mille family who had acted as lawyers and stewards for the Priory of St. Swithun, and perhaps also for the Priory of Breamore, acquired more

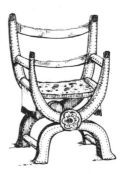

Queen Mary's Chair, Winchester Cathedral

*Sir William Paulet,
K.G., 1st Marquess of
Winchester*

town property as well as a large estate on the western side of Southampton Water. John Mille (? 1509–1551) was Town Clerk and Recorder, and the ancestor of a well-known Hampshire family, the Barker Mills, whose property came to include the manors of Eling, Millbrook, Langley, Colbury, and Mottisfont. Typical also of the new men of the Reformation was the first Marquess of Winchester, William Paulet (d. 1572), whose great estate in Hampshire was widespread, although partly as the result of inheritance from the de Port family, including the great house at Basing soon to be the centre of Royalist resistance in the Civil War of Charles I's time. All the new Tudor landlords were in fact bound by the most practical considerations to be obedient to the monarch, and therefore to the Protestant Reformation. The first Marquess of Winchester, when asked how he survived the various political and religious changes of each reign replied that he had been a willow and not an oak. It is arguable as to how much economic change the new landlords brought to the county. There was economic distress and unemployment in late-16th-century Hampshire, but these were results of many factors, not just of the Reformation and the dissolution of the monasteries. The breakdown of the old system of training in craft gilds, the increased number of industrial capitalists, which made it hard for a man to set up on his own, and the number of soldiers and sailors returning from the wars all produced social difficulties, which were accentuated by inflation. The government relied on Justices of the Peace to deal with unemployed and vagrant men and women, and in 1578 a large 'House of Correction' was set up for the county in Winchester, under the supervision of the county magistrates. to provide training and supervision for all whom they sent there. In some parts of England the Reformation resulted in the enclosure of much land and a tendency to change from arable to sheep farming. Hampshire was already predominantly a sheep county, and the enclosure movement had begun before the Reformation according to Wolsey's commission of 1517, south Hampshire being enclosed earlier than the rest of the county. The greatest single example of enclosure in 1517 was of 120 acres at Bramshill where, about 100 years later, one of Hampshire's great country houses was built, in brick, material whose rediscovery did much to affect the architectural appearance of the county. Grove Place, at Nursling, near Southampton, also in brick, was built at the end of the 16th century by the son of a London merchant who had profited by the Reformation, and has a formal garden of typical Tudor design.

The county's most famous house, The Vyne, at Sherborne St. John, belongs to the early Tudor period and was built by the first Lord Sandys, in diapered red brick with stone ornamentaion and sculptured

70

coats of arms of Henry VIII and Catherine of Aragon and the owner himself, who was perhaps noticed by Anne Boleyn when she visited The Vyne with the king in October 1535. Lord Sandys was a member of an ancient Hampshire family, a loyal subject of the king and not greatly involved in the religious changes of the time. An inventory of The Vyne made after his death in 1541 provides a fascinating account of the household of a great Hampshire nobleman of the period, describing each room, its contents, Lord Sandys's horses, his household linen, his jewels and his plate, as well as the contents of his personal wardrobe. His support of the ancient faith did not, however, prevent him from converting Mottisfont Priory into a secondary residence. A later member of the Sandys family entertained Elizabeth I at The Vyne in 1569 with much difficulty and great expense.

Warblington Castle

By this time, the Anglican Church settlement was more or less established but the extreme Protestant policy of Bishop Horne (1561–80) provoked much bitterness in a diocese which had been comparatively undisturbed by the Marian persecutions, and which had produced only one martyr, the Archdeacon of Winchester, John Philpot of Compton who was burnt at Smithfield in 1555. Horne destroyed all those parts of the cathedral fabric which seemed 'superstitious', windows of medieval glass, the surviving statues, and the great rood. He endeavoured to enforce the punishment of recusants, those Roman Catholics who would not attend the services of the Established Church, and many were subject to heavy nominal fines which were never in fact actually collected. The Hampshire families known to be recusants included the Cottons of Warblington, the Shelleys at Buriton, and some of the Paulets. Much more serious than non-attendance at church was the crime of denying the royal supremacy, and for this, two Hampshire men, John Slade and John Body, suffered the fate of traitors in 1583, Slade at Winchester, Body at Andover. Their deaths were undoubtedly intended as a warning, for the old religion remained strong in certain towns, particularly in Winchester. Religious difficulties, unemployment, political uncertainty and financial crises as well as fear of foreign invasion were the problems facing many men and women at the end of the 16th century. Those who suffered in the hundred years after Henry VIII reformed the Church included many close to the throne; Margaret de la Pole, whose Hampshire home was Warblington Castle, and several members of the widespread Seymour family.

The Netley foundation inscription

XII Tudor Towns

Hurst Castle

The military and naval activity of the Hundred Years War brought varying degrees of temporary prosperity to Hampshire towns. Both Portsmouth and Southampton suffered in the long wars with France when both were burnt, and the constitutional development of the former was hampered to a certain extent by Southampton's claim to consider Portsmouth a mere part of its own greater port and not an independent town. The county was not the scene of major fighting in the Wars of the Roses, yet the Tudor period which followed, was often a time of financial difficulty for some corporations, despite the individual prosperity of many townsmen. There is a marked contrast between the wealth of individuals and the general complaints of decay and financial hardship drawn up often by the very same men on behalf of their own boroughs.

Henry VII's decision to build a dry dock at Portsmouth in 1495 was a decisive factor in the town's future history. Though this dock was soon filled in, and though during the reign of Elizabeth I the harbour was used by many pirates, and there was also much secret coming and going on the part of Roman Catholic priests and recusants, and though royal interest centred on seaports nearer London or on the activities of West Country seamen, Portsmouth's place in national history as a permanent home for the Navy was soon established without doubt. In 1600, a royal charter from the queen gave Portsmouth its first definite status as a corporate borough, under a mayor elected by the burgesses. Its importance as a naval centre and garrison town was shown by the fact that the grant was not in any way to prejudice the power of the Captain of Portsmouth. In 1627 Charles I confirmed all these privileges, granting the inhabitants also the right of making certain kinds of woollen cloth, an indication that the town's prosperity was not entirely bound up with the future of the Royal Navy. Law and order were maintained by the court-leet which dealt with all trading offences as well as frequent complaints of 'fray and bloodshed'. Religious life centred round the original Portsmouth parish church of St. Thomas (now the cathedral) and the church of St. Mary at Kingston, which had belonged to Southwick Priory until its dissolution in 1539.

In contrast to Portsmouth, in the Tudor and early Stuart period, Southampton's fortunes were declining. By 1531 the Corporation there was almost bankrupt, chiefly because of the absence of foreign trade. The effect of the withdrawal of the Venetian galleys was particularly noticeable, and not until the 19th century did trade with the New World recreate the town's former commercial prosperity. Yet there were wealthy men in the Tudor town, chiefly 'new' men who had founded their fortunes as a result of the economic changes brought about by the Reformation. Amongst these were the Mille or Mills family, Town Clerks and Recorders, who were able to speculate in Southampton and Hampshire property and soon set themselves up as landed gentry, with a town house in the High Street and fine manor houses on the other side of Southampton Water.

Seal of Southampton, 1588

The early Tudor period in Winchester was a time of financial difficulty in civic affairs. The Corporation attempted to meet this problem by obtaining a series of reductions in the fee-farm of the city and by obtaining permission for the mayor to take his oath of office locally instead of having to go to London with a retinue at the citizens' expense. A more positive and very special kind of financial help was given after the marriage of Philip and Mary in Winchester Cathedral, an event which required considerable local expenditure. A series of Letters Patent granted Winchester various reductions in the city's fee-farm and also gave the Corporation those properties in the city which had formerly belonged to certain dissolved monastic houses. Like Portsmouth, Winchester obtained its first charter of incorporation from Elizabeth I and this great charter set out Winchester's constitution as it had evolved from medieval times. Local government under a mayor and corporation of 24 survived undisturbed until the Municipal Corporations Act of 1835, despite attacks from the later Stuarts.

The governments of Southampton, Portsmouth and Winchester were essentially plutocratic, but these local men occasionally needed help from a social level higher than any they themselves could hope to reach. Thus in Portsmouth, the Corporation obtained the good services of Lord Mountjoy, Captain of the port there, in order to petition Elizabeth I for that charter granted in 1600. In Southampton, the Corporation approached Sir Francis Walsingham when they needed a friend at Court, and Walsingham was made Winchester's first High Steward for exactly the same practical consideration. A 'new' man himself, he thus succeeded to the position of a powerful local patron, similar to that enjoyed in medieval times by some of Hampshire's feudal nobility, including the bishops of the diocese and the lay Justices of Assize.

Despite certain economic difficulties, there were in fact many prosperous Hampshire townsfolk. Some could afford to build themselves fine town houses and where these survive, in a few places only,

Sir Francis Walsingham

73

*'Tudor House',
Southampton*

they are the best possible proof of the prosperity of Tudor Hampshire. The timber-framed building called 'Tudor House' in St. Michael's Square, Southampton, was built by Sir John Dawtrey, a royal customs official who was Sheriff of Hampshire in 1516. Wills and inventories provide many details of other houses. In the reign of Elizabeth I, Winchester was something of a centre for medical studies, and John Warner, dean from 1559 till 1564, had been first Regius Professor of Medicine. Doctor Thomas Bassett, who died in 1575, had a fine house with many rooms including a hall, a parlour furnished with joined table and stools, cushions of tapestry and needlework, a study containing a standing glass for a student, that is, a microscope, and a dispensary complete with still, at the back of the building. It is not certain where Bassett's house stood, but Doctor Simon Trippe, who was physician to the Dean and Chapter of Winchester till his death in 1586, had an even more elaborate and finely-furnished establishment in what is now Colebrook House. Trippe was a Renaissance gentleman, educated at Oxford, Cambridge, and Padua.

Occasionally large new Tudor houses encroached on what had been ancient lanes and rights of way. Thus in 1582 the construction of a great town mansion by Sir Walter Sandys, in charge of the Winchester garrison, meant the partial but permanent closing of the south end of Lower Brook Street in Winchester. At the western end of the south side of the High Street, the Bethell family entirely enclosed St. Nicholas' Lane for the same sort of purpose. The Bethells' main residence, Hyde House, on the outskirts of Winchester, was built in the new material, brick, and on the ancient site of Hyde Abbey which the family had eventually obtained from Wriothesley after the dissolution of the monastery.

A general use of brick, instead of wattle and daub, began to transform the appearance of many street frontages. The average house still occupied the site of its medieval predecessor, but increased space was sometimes obtained, as it is now, by building high. A town house which belonged to the Dean and Chapter of Winchester Cathedral, the old Manor of God-be-got, was thus rebuilt as one of the tallest timber-framed brick buildings in central Winchester, with fine stone fireplaces, and can be compared with Moberly's in Kingsgate Street built in 1571.

It would be wrong indeed to leave the Tudor period without a brief glimpse of the very large number of charitable bequests which are such a feature of that age, some carrying on old medieval traditions, but others, with their main emphasis on education and indicative of a concern for learning. Peter Symonds left money for the almshouses called Christ's Hospital, and in Winchester, also, Ralph Lamb rebuilt the

*The Seal of the
City of Winchester*

almshouses of St. John's Hospital. At Andover a free school was founded by John Hanson in 1571, the founder and first headmaster both being Wykehamists. At Southampton a grammar school was founded with money left for the purpose by William Capon who had been rector of St. Mary's, and who died in 1550. Many townspeople were not only prosperous, but also public-spirited and had a conscious civic pride, a pride expressed also in corporate improvements in the general standards of town life, sanitary conditions, street lighting, for example, and a pride also expressed in the frequent and not always successful attempts to make compulsory the wearing of special gowns and hats by senior members of civic corporations.

This prosperity of professional men, lawyers, doctors, schoolmasters, was to a certain extent a contrast with the prosperity of medieval towns, which was centred particularly on direct commercial activity and the profits of retail and wholesale trading; it was the source, not only of wealth, but of much of the opposition to the first Stuart kings of England.

A Tichborne spoon

75

XIII Civil War and Social Change

Sir William Waller

The first two Stuart kings of England were often in Hampshire before the outbreak of the Civil War in 1642. In 1603, James I came to Winchester during Sir Walter Raleigh's trial for treason, and his son, Charles, Prince of Wales, was given a great welcome at Portsmouth in 1623, for the inhabitants were delighted that he had not succeeded in winning the hand of a Spanish princess. Charles stayed in Southampton, as king, in 1625 and in 1627 and was well received, yet there can be no doubt that his marriage with a Roman Catholic French princess, his religious and financial policies as well as his attempt to rule arbitrarily without a parliament made him very unpopular with many of his Hampshire subjects. When the Civil War broke out in 1642, Hampshire, like many of the English counties, had no hard or fast divisions of classes or districts between king and parliament. Winchester was famous for its loyalty to the Crown, yet even in that city there were prominent 'Puritans' who disliked the reform of the Church begun by Archbishop Laud, a reform associated in Hampshire with the Dean of Winchester, John Young and Lancelot Andrewes, whom James I made Bishop of Winchester. In Southampton, the Pilgrim Fathers had not been unwelcome when they gathered there to sail from the port in 1620, taking a local youth among the crew; 20 years later that town gave a great welcome to William Prynne the Puritan writer and pamphleteer, on his return from imprisonment in the Channel Islands. There can be little doubt that there were many Hampshire men who felt that they must oppose the king for reasons of religious conscience.

The chief Royalist leader in Hampshire was John Paulet, Marquess of Winchester, whose headquarters were at Basing House, the greatest Royalist strong point in the county. Other county Royalist families included the Tichbornes, the Sandys of Mottisfont and of The Vyne, the Oglanders of the Isle of Wight, and the commander of the Winchester garrison, Sir William Ogle, but amongst the gentry there were many painful divisions. The parliamentarian general, Sir William Waller, was a cousin of the loyal Marquess, and brother-in-law to Sir William Ogle. One of the Tichbornes moved far enough away from the family pattern to become parliamentary lord mayor of London and to sign Charles I's death warrant. Other county gentlemen who fought against the king included the Flemings of North Stoneham,

76

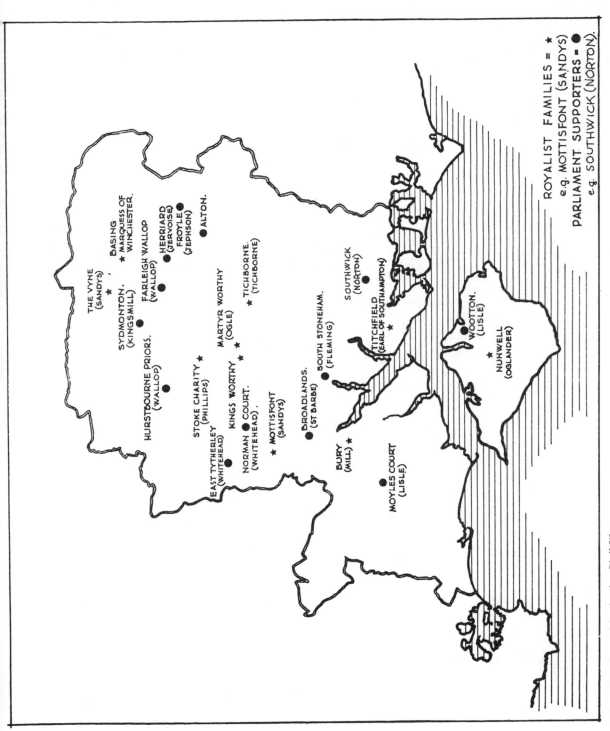

Map 10. Hampshire in the Civil War.

ROYALIST FAMILIES = ★
e.g. MOTTISFONT (SANDYS)
PARLIAMENT SUPPORTERS = ●
e.g. SOUTHWICK (NORTON).

THE VYNE
(SANDYS)
★

BASING
★
MARQUESS OF
WINCHESTER.

SYDMONTON.
(KINGSMILL)
★

FARLEIGH WALLOP
(WALLOP)
★

HERRIARD
(JERVOISE)
★

FROYLE
(JEPHSON)
●

ALTON.
●

HURSTBOURNE PRIORS.
(WALLOP)
★

STOKE CHARITY
(PHILLIPS)
★

MARTYR WORTHY
(OGLE)
★

TICHBORNE.
(TICHBORNE)
●

EAST TYTHERLEY
(WHITEHEAD)
●

KINGS WORTHY
★

NORMAN COURT.
(WHITEHEAD).
●

MOTTISFONT
(SANDYS)
★

BROADLANDS.
(ST BARBE)

SOUTH STONEHAM.
(FLEMING)
●

SOUTHWICK
(NORTON)
●

TITCHFIELD
(EARL OF SOUTHAMPTON)
★

BURY
(MILL)
★

MOYLES COURT
(LISLE)
●

WOOTTON
(LISLE)
●

NUNWELL
(OGLANDER)
●

77

Richard Cromwell

Colonel Norton of Old Alresford and Southwick Park, and Francis St. Barbe of Broadlands near Romsey.

In both Southampton and Portsmouth there was strong feeling for parliament. Both had suffered from the burdens of forced loans, from the imposition of ship money, and from the billeting of royal troops. Soon after the outbreak of war both towns capitulated to parliamentarian demands, and their loss to the king was a vital factor in the eventual defeat of the Royalist forces. Roughly speaking it is perhaps true to suggest that the western half of the county was more Royalist than the east. Support for parliament was strong in the Isle of Wight, and particularly associated with John Lisle of Wootton and his family, though a number of local gentlemen headed by John Oglander, Lisle's godfather, were known to be Royalists.

The surrender of Portsmouth and Southampton, a temporary taking of Winchester, and the slighting of Farnham Castle, home of the diocesan bishop, were all early indications of the way in which the war was eventually to go. In 1644 the Royalists suffered a further great defeat at Cheriton. Cheriton was followed by the appearance of Oliver Cromwell on the Hampshire scene, by the surrender of Winchester to him in 1645, and by the fall of Basing House and its almost complete demolition. In 1647 the king became a prisoner in the Isle of Wight at Carisbrooke Castle, whence he was eventually moved to Hurst Castle. On his journey through the county, to his trial at London, Charles was received with courage and with loyalty by the Winchester Corporation at the Westgate of the city. At nearby Hursley, the squire of the village, Richard Major, was a personal friend of Oliver Cromwell, and Major's daughter, Dorothy, married the Lord Protector's son, Richard. It thus happened that after the Restoration Oliver's grandchildren lived quietly in this Hampshire village.

The Restoration of the monarchy in 1660 was undoubtedly a popular event in Hampshire. Many people had lost all for the king or parliament's sake, and looked forward, in some cases in vain, to a period of restitution and political stability. Sir John Mill, at whose Southampton house the king had dined in 1627, had a son killed at Oxford and was himself ruined by the war, falsely accused of being a Papist, and had his personal property, including the family plate, stripped from him by looting soldiers. He died before the Restoration, with little indeed to leave to his family. The Paulets and the Tichbornes were temporarily ruined. Amongst the king's supporters Arthur Capell, of Martyr Worthy, was beheaded in Whitehall in March 1649. Sir John Oglander of Nunwell was almost ruined, was frequently arrested and imprisoned, and his children on the mainland

Basing House

found it impossible to visit him for the double fear of leaving their homes to be rifled by the army or of meeting with soldiers on their way to Nunwell. Between 1642 and 1645 the countryside suffered greatly from the almost constant marching and counter marching of the armies of the Crown and of parliament, the billeting of soldiers and the general ravages of war; a contemporary observer in 1644 describes Hampshire as practically ruined with nothing left in it for man or beast. One of the saddest aspects of the war was the divisions which it brought into family life. Sir John Oglander had a parliamentarian brother, and his cousin and godson, John Lisle of Wootton in the Isle of Wight (member of parliament for Winchester in 1642) was a Cromwellian. Yet all was not bitterness or loss. The close tie of kinship which bound so many of the Hampshire families had a softening influence. Even such an important Hampshire change as the sale of the Sandys' great house of The Vyne to Challoner Chute in 1653 had its mitigating factors, for Chute was acknowledged as the most eminent lawyer in England, and though later to be well known as Speaker of Richard Cromwell's House of Commons he was gratefully remembered in Royalist circles as the advocate who had dared in 1641 to defend 'the Bishops of England in their extreme peril' as well as Archbishop Laud two years later.

King Charles I

Royalist military failure, the legislation of the Long and Rump parliaments and the death of the king brought therefore many changes to Hampshire. The Bishop of Winchester's castles at Wolvesey and at nearby Farnham in Surrey were 'slighted'; Winchester Castle was virtually demolished and Sir William Waller, who claimed it in his own right, eventually sold the great hall to a group of trustees for the county. The Dean and Chapter of Winchester were abolished, the cathedral left to the preaching and services of ministers, of whom one, Theophilus Gale, a brilliant scholar, eventually founded that Dissenting academy at Stoke Newington which later on had as one of its pupils the most famous of Free Church hymn-writers, Isaac Watts of Southampton. Throughout the county, the Dean and Chapter's many estates were let out to new tenants, the cathedral became dilapidated and was almost demolished in 1653, and the Close was so ruined that much of it had to be pulled down or rebuilt after 1660. The parliamentarian inhabitants of the Close in 1649 included two 'ministers' and John Lisle, the city's Recorder.

Isaac Watts, 1674–1748

A brief word only need be said of Hampshire in the later years of the 17th century. Both Winchester and Southampton were involved in the constitutional difficulties with Charles II and James II, and both towns lost their charters.

An extravagant scheme begun by Charles II for making Winchester again the royal capital with a great Versailles type of palace designed

The Pilgrims' Memorial

by Sir Christopher Wren, and actually begun in 1683, was virtually abandoned in the reign of George I, and the building, left uncompleted, became the nucleus of Winchester barracks.

Though Hampshire was not concerned in the Monmouth rebellion, John Lisle's widow, Dame Alicia Lisle of Moyle's Court, in the New Forest, was accused of harbouring rebels at her home after the defeat at Sedgemoor. She was tried by Judge Jeffreys, and executed in the Square in Winchester in 1685. At this notorious trial attempts were made to pack the jury, and to terrify the townspeople by billeting soldiers on them. It was a Winchester member of a very famous Hampshire family, Thomas Wavell, who encouraged his fellow citizens to resist James II's attempts at arbitrary government, though local liberty might have suffered a permanent setback had not the king been forced to flee the country in 1688.

One of the most important results of these failures of royal attempts at arbitrary government was eventually the growth of a strong local government based on democratic local responsibility. Much of this local government, in town and country alike, was carried out by Justices of the Peace. Justices supervised the records of the parish 'overseers of the poor' who had to collect local poor rates and apprentice poor children: they saw, too, that each local parish surveyor kept his roads in fair repair. Meeting at Quarter Sessions, County Justices supervised the repairs of the County Hall within Winchester Castle, provided accommodation for judges and juries, administered the county jail, suppressed poaching, and administered the few national taxes, for example the Land Tax and the better known Window Tax of William and Mary's reign, which is always blamed for many blocked windows in large houses.

In 1662 a large number of laymen and over 2,000 beneficed clergymen in England, unable to accept the liturgy of the new Prayer Book of that year, left the Anglican Church. It is significant that it was the justices, all members of the Established Church, who were given the task of licensing the 'Dissenters' chapels which soon sprang up all over the county. By the end of the 17th century, Quarter Sessions records show that there was little persecution in Hampshire of either Dissenters or Roman Catholics. An era of difficulties and of political and religious conflict gave way, by the beginning of Queen Anne's reign, to a period of tolerance and political quiet.

21. The giving of the dole: Sir Henry Tichborne, his family and the villagers in *c.* 1670; from the painting by Gillis van Tilborch.

22. (*right*) 17th-century plaque recording Bishop Morley's foundation of his college for the widows of clergymen.

23. (*above*) Whitchurch town hall, *c.* 1708.

24. (*left*) Portsmouth town hall, *c.* 1739.

25. Market Place, Bishop's Waltham, *c.* 1840.

26. Portsmouth in 1714.

27. Bere Mill.

28. Machinery in Bere Mill.

XIV The 18th Century: Peaceful Change, Corruption, and Social Conscience

In the early years of the 18th century Hampshire towns were in decline: Daniel Defoe, writing of Winchester in *c.* 1720, described the city as a place of no trade, and Southampton as 'a truly ancient town . . . dying with age'. Portsmouth (and presumably he had not heard of the corruption of the Corporation), he found flourishing, taking note, however, of Camden's verdict that 'Portsmouth flourished in time of war but not in time of peace'. He was a townsman; the New Forest horrified him with its wasted and undeveloped land, and unlike later travellers through the county, particularly Arthur Young, William Marshall and Charles Vancouver, he was not really interested in the many agricultural changes that were taking place and bringing some measure of prosperity to Hampshire farmers, for as the century progressed the agriculture of the county was improved. An important part of this change was the enclosure movement, enclosures for improvement, not just for sheep-farming as they had been in the Tudor period; and carried out by mutual consent, by Act of Parliament or illegally. The great open fields of medieval Hampshire gradually disappeared, and small farmers were often swallowed up by richer landlords, for enclosure could be an expensive process. Crops and stocks changed, and machinery was introduced into a way of life which had relied almost entirely on the labour of men's hands. One of the earliest farmers to improve his crops and to vary them was Edward Lisle of Crux Easton, in the north of Hampshire, who grew turnips and new grains, rape grass, clover, and sanfoin, and who used malt dust as a fertiliser, but it appears to have been the south which was enclosed before the rest of the county. Crown lands there were in poor condition, and in the New Forest there were too many deer and not enough good timber for the Royal Navy. Even in Vancouver's time, however (*c.* 1817), a large area around Portsmouth still preserved the open three-field system, though much of the fallow was being used for market gardening. Roots were being grown everywhere, turnips, swedes and kohl-rabi, and regional specialities included the hops of the Alton–Farnham area, and cabbages grown for the prevention of scurvy amongst patients in the Royal Naval hospital founded at Haslar in 1744.

H.M.S. Victory

81

Tichborne church

Agricultural implements changed, too, but only very wealthy landlords could afford the new threshing mills Vancouver noted at Abbotstone, Twyford and Tichborne. There were almost as many varieties of plough as there were varieties of Hampshire land, and there was no indigenous breed of cattle. Special milking varieties were introduced very slowly: when Jane Austen was a child her father kept five Alderney cows at Steventon. Vancouver found Guernsey cattle at Lymington and Milford, and in 1817 an Ovington farmer advertised a few Alderney cows for sale in the *Hampshire Chronicle*. Hampshire horses were not considered to be very good, but pigs were improved by cross-breeding; as far as sheep were concerned the county had been divided into two sections at the villages of East and West Meon, but the small heath sheep of the west disappeared and the Southdown flocks from the east spread along the chalk hills. Prominent owners like Sir Henry Tichborne and Thomas Miller owned famous flocks.

All these changes in agriculture were accompanied by another quiet revolution, the changes in transport, which made it possible for surplus crops and stock bred for a market to be moved from producer to consumer with increasing rapidity. Change came first to roads and to bridges, and there were attempts to provide canals, though Hampshire was never a canal county. Many of the bridges over the Test were built or rebuilt in the late 18th century, and the county justices spent money regularly on those bridges which served county traffic, Redbridge, Fordingbridge, Christchurch, Ringwood, and Stockbridge. Improvements to main roads were usually financed by money collected at tollgates and turnpikes set up under a long series of Acts of Parliament, and a number of these rather picturesque toll houses survive. In towns, Paving Commissioners, also set up under Acts of Parliament, slowly improved local roads, made pavements, licensed sedan chairs and hackney carriages, and controlled alterations to all house frontages, including the making of bow windows.

There were still the occasional highwaymen, like the Golden Farmer of northern Hampshire, but facilities for travellers improved greatly as the century continued, and many coaching inns like the *Black Swan,* the *White Hart,* and the *George* in Winchester, the *Dolphin* in Southampton, and the *George* at Portsmouth became nationally famous. Even small towns were linked by regular services, and a *Guide to Coaches,* published in 1753, gives a long list of towns in alphabetical order with the names of the London inns from which their services started. The first regular coach service from Southampton to London had begun in 1720, and the Southampton *Guide* of 1774 describes the many services available to the travelling public, setting out usually under 'Mr. Rogers'' direction to London via Hook and Holborn, to

82

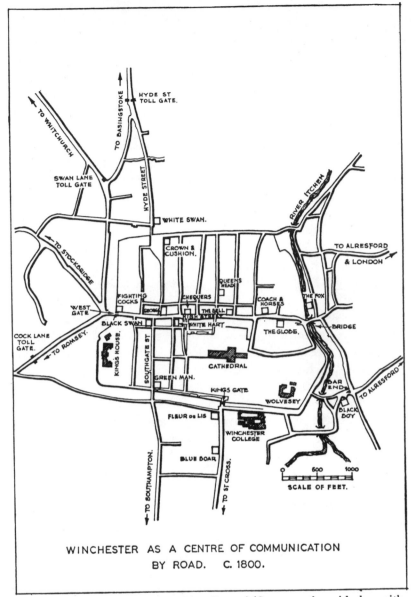

WINCHESTER AS A CENTRE OF COMMUNICATION
BY ROAD.   C. 1800.

Map 11.   Winchester as a Coaching Centre' (Compare the grid plan with
that of Silchester, p. 20.)

Lymington, and to Gosport and Salisbury. Coach travel was expensive
and the travelling poor went on foot, by horse, or by carriers' wagon.
Amongst the most successful Hampshire carriers were the Waldrons of
Winchester and the Asletts and Harpers of Southampton; Collyer's
'Reading Wagons' took goods across the county border from Southampton on to Reading, and then to Birmingham. Letters could be carried
by the coaches of the Royal Mail from about 1784 onwards, and the
postage on a letter from Southampton to London was fourpence. By
1790 the most luxurious public vehicle on the Hampshire roads was

Collyer's 'Flying Machine on steel springs, with a guard', which left the *Star* inn at Southampton every weekday at 5 a.m., for *The Belle Savage* on Ludgate Hill. Some members of Gilbert White's family were very interested in travelling; a nephew went in the first carriage which travelled up Stonor Hill on the new Petersfield road in 1826, and a great nephew, the diarist, Edmund Yalden White, curate of Crondall, recorded the death of 'Mr. Collyer, the Great Coach Proprietor' in 1836. Faster speeds brought their inevitable increase in traffic accidents: the Alton coach overturned on 24 July 1823 because one horse had staggers, and the day after the Birmingham coach overturned with fatal results when a wheel came off.

It was unfortunate that these improvements, the so-called peaceful revolution in Hampshire agriculture and transport, brought prosperity to only a few; the situation of the mass of the people was often miserable and poverty-stricken, and made worse by political corruption.

Most Hampshire men had found it easy to accept the peaceful accession of George I, for the county had had enough of civil war and change by violent political revolution. In 1717 the Grand Jury of Hampshire presented the Warden, Fellows, Master, Usher and Children of Winchester College for their known disaffection and corruption of manners; the school was rightly suspected of Jacobite leanings. The number of commoner boys was only 12, for county gentlemen were hesitating to send their sons to such a notorious place, and later on there were county petitions drawn up 'against' the Jacobite Rebellion in 1745 and the French Revolution. It was easier to secure allegiance for a cause through men's pockets than by appealing to their principles.

There is plenty of evidence for the extent of political corruption in 18th-century Hampshire. In the town, the right to vote was restricted to a small number of freemen, whose votes could be bought and sold, and who were subject, if they were tradesmen, to the political pressures of their most important customers. In 1705 the then mayor of Winchester, John Penton, managed to get the Common Assembly to agree to a resolution that in future freemen were to be chosen only at the November assembly, on pain of the mayor being fined £30 for such transgression; but this reform did not last, and the two local dukes, Bolton (of Abbotstone and Hackwood) and Chandos (from Avington Park) managed the Corporation in their own interests until 1835. In Portsmouth, the Corporation was subject to pressure from the Admiralty, and reform was achieved by the rather dubious efforts of the Carter family. In 1750, John Carter, a wealthy dissenter, secured at a meeting in his own home the election of 62 burgesses, of whom 18 were children, including Carter's own two sons, aged eight and

John Carter,
1715-1794

84

five. There was trouble about this, and the Admiralty party applied economic pressure by threatening to withdraw naval contracts, but from 1782 onwards the Carter family ruled the town and corruption died away; another result, eventually, was the emergence of the family (as Bonham-Carters) as a major political influence in national affairs. In Southampton the Corporation evolved a method of preventing change and helping its finances by creating burgesses, men of fortune from the surrounding countryside, who were prepared to give donations to local causes as well as to the Corporation's funds direct. This apparently lessened the supply of 'unsuitable' parliamentary candidates and the chances of disputed elections, but Southampton was very corrupt. Anthony Henley, one of the two members of parliament in 1733, was asked by his constituents to vote against Walpole's Excise Bill, and replied to their letter in no uncertain terms . . . 'You know what I know very well, that I bought you . . . and I know what perhaps you think I don't know, you are now selling yourselves to somebody else. And I know, what you don't know, that I am buying another borough'. Peter Delmé, M.P. in 1747, who had bought the Cams estate near Fareham, paid £500 to become a freeman of Southampton. Amongst the smaller Hampshire towns Stockbridge was notorious. By 1689, a vote there cost between four and six guineas: by 1784 it was established as an 'open borough', that is, not one in the pocket of some great lord, but one where anyone could get elected provided he paid the Bailiff a sum larger than that of his opponents. The general election of 1790 was particularly notorious, and evidence given before a Select Committee of the House of Commons revealed that the price per vote was 70 guineas to each elector. In the event, a Bill proposed to prevent bribery and corruption in Stockbridge never became law, and by 1816 the electors were still expecting £60 a vote, and a successful candidate in 1831 in fact paid £1,000 for his seat.

Hampshire towns were not the only seats of bribery and corruption. Until 1884, when Gladstone brought in single-member constituencies, the county returned two members (the old Knights of the Shires) chosen by Hampshire freemen at a kind of election in the Great Hall of Winchester Castle. Whoever brought the greater number of supporters won the day: county members were inevitably 'court nominees', as a writer in the *Victoria County History* describes them: in 1780 'anyone may be chosen for Hampshire that the government pleases without trouble or expense'.

Yet it was not because men were without social consciences that political life in Hampshire was so corrupt. It was a malaise of the age. Life was still rough and harsh for many people, to be improved only

The Grange, at Northington

85

The 1st Duke of Wellington

by the possession of money. Social change came with economic change in the county, but many of the most important economic changes brought misery for ordinary people, and it was not until the last quarter of the century that Hampshire towns began once more to prosper. Even then, some of this prosperity was false, brought about by the long wars with France which prevented the import of cheap food, encouraged the industries of war, and eventually prepared a recipe for social disaster by a series of repressive Acts of Parliament which forbade men to assemble in public meetings, forbade the formation of trade unions, censored the press, and restricted the freedom of family life for the poor and needy. Recruiting for the war with France by press gang and with men under the influence of drink was usual; the army and the navy continued (until 1884) to discipline its rank and file by flogging, and there were serious mutinies and desertions. When Anson began his voyage round the world from Portsmouth in 1740 the authorities had to make up his numbers with 500 invalids, out-pensioners from Chelsea, and of these more than half who had the strength to walk out of the town deserted. The great mutiny at Spithead in 1797 was brought about by very real grievances: poor pay and insufficient food.

By the end of the first quarter of the 19th century standards of living in the Hampshire countryside were poor, and much criticised by one of the most vehement radicals of the time, William Cobbett (1763–1835), journalist, politician and unsuccessful farmer, the self-taught son of a farm labourer. Like Defoe, Cobbett rode all over Hampshire, but unlike the earlier writer he was a countryman born and bred, and his *Rural Rides* are essential reading for anyone interested in this period of Hampshire history. He was a defender of the rights of the people, the champion of the English yeoman. He disliked paper money, and the Hampshire family who manufactured it, 'Squire Portal of Rag Castle'; he suspected absentee landlords, amongst them the Ogles of Worthy Park, and was suspicious, too, of the Baring family because he felt that they probably used their money to apply political pressures disguised as social relief. He disliked the first Duke of Wellington, in many ways an admirable landlord; though as a farmer himself at Botley Cobbett was a failure. The labouring classes viewed with increasing anxiety the important changes which made up the agricultural revolution, and Cobbett urged them on. In 1830 there were widespread agricultural riots in the county, followed by famous trials, and some men were hung and many more transported.

Cobbett edited a famous newspaper, *The Political Register,* and in the development of Hampshire's social conscience a new phenomenon, the local newspaper, played a fair part. Local papers with long

Hale Park

histories, and still in existence, include the *Salisbury and Winchester Journal,* established in Salisbury in 1729, and the *Hampshire Chronicle,* the county newspaper, first printed in Southampton in 1772 but published from 1778 in Winchester. Such papers were rarely sensational or lurid, even when reporting serious crime, like the affair of Jack the Painter who set fire to Portsmouth Dockyard in 1776 because he was in sympathy with the American revolution. The painter's body hung in chains on Portsmouth front, and public executions were the order of the day. Women convicted of poisoning their husbands were still burnt alive, and in 1784 the execution of Mary Bayley, who was burnt at the stake about a mile out of Winchester on the Newbury road, attracted a vast crowd of spectators.

It was a rough, harsh world, but a society which produced in 1736 the first county hospital set up outside London, innumerable village schools and individuals who gave large sums to charitable causes, a society which cared for prisoners of war, and even refugee Papist priests, was neither uncaring nor uncivilised. The Hampshire County hospital was founded by Alured Clarke, a Canon of the Cathedral, and though the Church in the 18th century has been much criticised, it was never wholly indifferent to the needs of its people. Gilbert White of Selborne (1720–93) was a good clergyman as well as a great naturalist, and even Philip Williams, absentee rector of Compton from 1781 to 1830, took care to arrange for the work of his parish.

There was probably never a time when 18th-century 'jobbery and snobbery' were the only contributions of the Hampshire gentry to local society, and though they can be criticised, the architectural inheritance of the county would be the poorer today had it not been for their good taste and learning. This is not the place to list Hampshire's 'stately homes', but Avington Park, The Vyne, and Hale Park are splendid examples, and on the smaller scale, Houghton Lodge is a kind of early Brighton Pavilion. The old town halls of Whitchurch, Winchester and Stockbridge and the smaller buildings of some of Hampshire's towns—Odiham, Bishop's Waltham, and Alresford, for example—show how the 18th-century style, so varied in application, spread, and shops of merchants and tradesmen have an elegance and simplicity never surpassed. In Southampton and Winchester the vast plate glass window of the 19th century was an architectural disaster, but there is still much to be admired at first-floor level. No. 105 Winchester High Street, now a bank, was designed by an unknown architect for a Hampshire apothecary in 1772; Minster House, in the same city was built as a bank; the offices of the *Hampshire Chronicle* still retain the dignity of their time; and Robert Mudie's charming views of c. 1840 show how much the county owes to the 18th century.

The Red Lion, *Petersfield*

XV Education, c. 1154-1976

The trusty servant

Comparatively little is known about the education of Hampshire children in the Middle Ages, but it is a fair assumption that there were always a number of town boys who were taught to read, write and calculate. It would be difficult otherwise to explain how the commercial life of the county flourished as it did, and by the 15th century even carters carrying their goods across Hampshire were able to write instructions for each other and for local officials. Nor was it unusual for benefit of clergy, which implies some measure of literacy, to be pled in the Courts. Village boys were taught to read and write, if they had some kind local patron or parish priest, and there must be hundreds of unrecorded examples of medieval children taught at home in a household where one literate parent realised the advantage of handing on a skill to his child. Simple reading can be taught on a slate with a piece of Hampshire chalk, or in sand: books are desirable, but not essential. Most wills were nuncupatory, communicated verbally on a death bed to the parish priest; there were few books, and few letters to write unless you were a highly successful merchant, and even then you could employ a clerk. Literacy was not necessarily a sign of status, and when the Accord of Winchester was signed in 1072— that great agreement which gave Canterbury precedence over York— William I and his Queen could only make their marks.

In 1295 a diocesan synod held in Winchester required all rectors, vicars and parish priests to make certain that the boys of their parishes were taught the Lord's Prayer, the Creed, the Hail Mary, how to sign themselves with the Cross, to read the Psalter, and how to sing; those boys would be suitable candidates for Holy Orders, though even then the standard was low. Most Hampshire priests were not university men, but peasants or artisans who had got by heart the Creed, the Ten Commandments, and the Holy Sacraments, as a minimum. A proportion of those who were ordained were allowed leave of absence to go to a university to study, even after their appointments to benefices, and the Winchester episcopal registers abound with examples of this kind of educational remedy long before William of Wykeham founded his great school. The prospect for girls was not so hopeful, and very few girls in medieval Hampshire were taught to read or write unless they came from gentle families, and then perhaps only a few. The nuns of St. Mary's Abbey and those in Romsey and

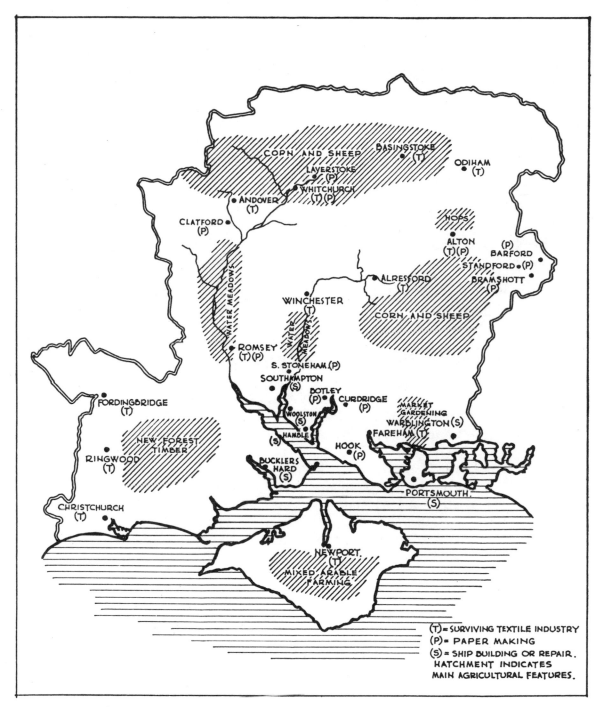

CORN AND SHEEP

BASINGSTOKE
(T)

ODIHAM
(T)

LAYERSTOKE
(P)

WHITCHURCH
(T)(P)

ANDOVER
(T)

CLATFORD
(P)

HOPS

ALTON
(T)(P)

BARFORD
(P)

STANDFORD
(P)

WATER MEADOWS

ALRESFORD
(T)

BRAMSHOTT
(P)

WINCHESTER
(T)

WATER MEADOWS

CORN AND SHEEP

ROMSEY
(T)(P)

S. STONEHAM (P)

SOUTHAMPTON
(S)

BOTLEY
(P)

CURDRIDGE
(P)

MARKET
GARDENING

FORDINGBRIDGE
(T)

WOOLSTON
(S)

WARBLINGTON (S)

FAREHAM (T)

NEW FOREST
TIMBER

HAMBLE
(S)

HOOK
(P)

RINGWOOD
(T)

BUCKLERS
HARD
(S)

PORTSMOUTH.
(S)

CHRISTCHURCH
(T)

NEWPORT.
(T)

MIXED ARABLE
FARMING

(T) = SURVIVING TEXTILE INDUSTRY
(P) = PAPER MAKING
(S) = SHIP BUILDING OR REPAIR.
HATCHMENT INDICATES
MAIN AGRICULTURAL FEATURES.

Map 12. Hampshire Industries, *c.* 1815

John Kent, a Winchester scholar

Wherwell did some teaching of their young lady boarders, who were not all intended for convent life, and in the later Middle Ages the monks of Hyde Abbey had a kind of preparatory school for boys. Cases of individual instruction apart, the Hampshire monasteries did not play a major part in the education of laymen. Cathedrals of the old foundation, like Salisbury, usually maintained a schoolmaster to teach boys who were not going into the Church. In Hampshire, by contrast, the monks of the great Benedictine churches taught only their novices. At the Cathedral the Almoner supplied these young men with presents, including their knife money, and there were seven youths in the Novices school in 1387, nine in 1459, none in 1485 or 1516: the promising young monks who went on to Gloucester Hall at Oxford were partly maintained from money supplied by the Priory Horderer, and there is more evidence to be found in the account rolls of other obedientiaries. It should not be thought, however, that all monks were literate. As late as 1387 Wykeham was complaining about illiteracy in St. Swithun's, and in 1497 a lay schoolmaster was appointed to 'inform the monks in grammar'. Apart from the novices there were usually a small group of boys whose job it was to sing, varying in number between four and 10 'boys of the Chapel', taught to sing and read, but not usually given any instruction in grammar or in Latin.

The foundation of Winchester College by William of Wykeham has proved to have educational results far beyond anything the founder might have imagined. 'St. Mary College near Winchester' was intended by the bishop to increase a steady supply of educated churchmen, most of whom would have continued their studies at his other foundation of New College, Oxford. High standards of attainment were required for entrance and are still required from any boy elected as one of the 70 scholars; commoner boys, too, were envisaged from the very beginnings in 1382, and the county was singularly fortunate in having such generous provision for its other children. Mr. T. Kirby's lists of Winchester Scholars (published in 1888), include boys from Kingsclere, Andover, Wickham, Romsey, Winchester, Stockbridge, Selborne, Alresford, and Alton in 1393, and Compton, Twyford, Overton, Winchester Soke in 1394. The college must have played an important part in the development of the idea of 'Hampshire'.

Hampshire boys who were not intending to become monks or priests were fortunate if they could come to Winchester, for the city had a very fine High Grammar School, traditionally said to have been the place of instruction of Anglo-Saxon kings. It was certainly in existence by the reign of Henry II, when its headmaster, Jordan Phantosme, obtained a prohibiton from the Pope forbidding his rival, John Joichel,

90

from teaching in the city. Thirteen poor scholars from this school were given a free midday meal each day in St. Cross hospital, with three quarts of beer per boy, and the boys were taught in a school-house on the western side of what is now Symonds Street, at the corner of Little Minster Lane. In 1544 this property was leased to the first Dean's mother, Alicia Tytheridge, but it was perhaps because the school was disused when Peter Symonds made his will in 1586 that he provided for the education of local poor boys, who were to live in his hospital. In the early 17th century a college usher, John Imber, was prevented from keeping a town school on the grounds that city boys were being taught in college. Individuals, like Lancelot Kirby the elder, kept private writing schools, and a well-known local doctor, William Over, founded (by will) the Winchester Free School in 1701. The most famous private school in Hampshire in the 18th century was probably that kept by Reynell Cotton, in Hyde Street, Winchester, where the pupils included the future Dean Garnier and future Prime Minister Canning, and where Cotton's successor, his son-in-law 'Bob' Richards, disciplined his boys by taking them to public hangings.

Other Hampshire towns were more fortunate after the Reformation, and the county soon had a number of excellent grammar schools, where teaching was based on the classics, where discipline was strict, and where instruction was confined to boys. William Capon left money to found such a school in Southampton in 1554 (King Edward VI); its most famous pupil in the 17th century was Isaac Watts, whose father kept a private school in the town. At Andover, a 'fre schole' was founded by a Wykehamist in 1571, John Hanson, whose bequest required that the schoolmaster should be a graduate. Alton had had a chantry school in 1472, founded by John Champfleur, but it had disappeared and was replaced by a successful Grammar School, Eggars, founded in 1638. Capon's school in Southampton had been preceded by a chantry foundation, also the case at Odiham. The Chantries Act of 1547 ended all these chantry schools and left gaps which could only be filled by private benefactors. Robert May founded a grammar school at Odiham in 1694, and at Bishop's Waltham, Bishop Morley, who purchased a fee farm rent worth £51 a year from the Crown in 1671 (derived from the site of the former Mottisfont Priory), used the income for various good purposes, including Morley College for Widowed Matrons in Winchester, and the paying of a schoolmaster in Bishop's Waltham. Some later charitable gifts increased this stipend, and like many other schools of its kind it inevitably became the responsibility of the incumbent of the parish, whose deputy taught the poor whilst he himself instructed a few fee-paying pupils who lived in the parsonage. This was happening at Bishop's Waltham in 1811,

George Morley,
Bishop, 1597–1684

91

Steventon church

and had happened in the household of Jane Austen's father at Steventon. Lymington, Ringwood and Alresford also had well-known grammar schools, but the most ancient of the local schools was that called the Holy Ghost school at Basingstoke, a name which survived the Reformation and was changed to Queen Mary's in 1886 (apparently for fear of sounding too Papist). Founded originally in *c.* 1524, it could probably claim to be the second oldest grammar school in the county; it has recently been reorganised. Portsmouth's school was a late foundation (1752); Alresford was older, but at its best in the 18th century; Christchurch had Richard Warner amongst its pupils.

All these schools offered an education based on the classics, not just the three Rs, and they provided education for middle-class boys. The school at Petersfield, founded under the will of Richard Churcher (1722), a successful East India merchant, and still known as Churcher's College, is a good example of how the commercial prosperity of interested Hampshire men encouraged them to think of boys who were likely to follow their founders' example. Here there was to be a lay headmaster (very unusual) whose pupils were to learn navigation and mathematics, with the object of becoming apprentices on ships sailing for the East Indies. Though an Act of Parliament in 1744 changed the scheme, and there were further changes in 1835 and 1876, Churcher's still remains an independent endowed school. Another school, founded at Southampton in 1752 under the will of Richard Taunton, a successful privateer, was primarily intended 'to fit children for the sea'; this has been reorganised under recent legislation.

The number of village 'primary' schools founded after the Reformation was not very large, though there are interesting examples at Broughton (1601, for 'reading, writing and casting'), Dummer (1610), and Kingsclere (1618), two small schools started during the Protectorate, Penton (1651) and Cliddesden (1656), and a village school began at Lyndhurst in 1668. In the next century, private enterprise and charity added to the number of village schools all over Hampshire, but there were some considerable gaps; the great period of foundation of what were soon to be called elementary schools belongs to the early 19th century, when the efforts of the two Societies, the National (Anglican) and the British and Foreign (Dissenters), gave Hampshire something like a nearly complete system of schools in towns and villages alike. The Education Act of 1870 filled the gaps by providing 'board schools', run by the State.

In the late 19th century many of the old grammar schools were considerably altered, and the Act of 1901 enabled the County Council to take a leading part in the establishment of state-aided girls' schools in Winchester, Gosport and Bournemouth. The Winchester Girls' High

92

School, now St. Swithun's, had already been set up by a group of private subscribers in 1884, and by that time there were opportunities for girls in the new State-provided elementary schools, although the provision of professional teacher-training in colleges was still restricted to male students for many years to come. The training of teachers was considered to be a rightful concern of the diocese, and the foundation of the Diocesan Training College (King Alfred's College) in Winchester in 1862 was a very important year in the history of education in Hampshire.

The training college had begun very modestly in 1838, with five students in 27/28 St. Swithun Street, Winchester, the object being to provide teachers who were 'humble, industrious, and instructive'. It was and is an Anglican foundation, one of 27 such colleges founded by the Church of England, and after having various homes was established on its present site in 1862, in a fine building designed by the Cathedral architect, John Colson, on the western side of Winchester. There have been many additions to this site in recent years, particularly as a result of the shortage of teachers after the Second World War. Expansion on a large scale began in 1958; the old two-year course was changed to three years, and women students were admitted. Ten years later there were about 750 students in King Alfred's. The recent decline in the number of teaching posts available has produced problems, and there have been suggestions of amalgamation, even closure, happily averted; King Alfred's is still training teachers, and also offers a B.A. course in History and English.

'K.A.C.' is older than Hampshire's own university at Southampton, which owes its foundation to the educational philosophy of a local man, Henry Robinson Hartley. He left a generous endowment in 1850, intended to encourage learning and culture in his native city, and though there was a long law suit, enough was left to found the Hartley Institute in Southampton in 1862. It became the Hartley University College in 1902, Southampton University College in 1914, and the University of Southampton in 1962, with a huge increase in the number of students and the kind of courses offered, and a great variety of new buildings of differing architectural styles. The term 'red-brick university' certainly no longer applies to Southampton.

The Diocesan Training College and the Hartley were successful. So, too, were the large number of Mechanics' Institutes founded after 1835, to instruct the working-class man in his spare time, providing reading rooms and libraries for those who could not buy books; they were the predecessors of today's Workers' Educational Association.

Most Hampshire children are now educated by the State, but this brief account of the development of education in the county would

Diocesan Training College, Winchester

Queenswood College

be incomplete if some mention were not made of the many educational opportunities provided by private enterprise. The 19th and 20th centuries abound with private schools and colleges of every possible variety. Some have achieved international fame, like Bedales, near Petersfield, the first co-educational boarding school. Others, like Queenswood College at East Tytherley, whose president was Robert Owen, the pioneer of the co-operative movement, proved short-lived. A series of major changes in Winchester College broadened the curriculum there, and sciences and mathematics (slowly) became important subjects; other schools were founded to cater for children whose parents wished them to be well-educated, but who could not afford to send them to boarding schools. Trafalgar House, in Winchester, seems to have been an excellent school of this kind, lasting from *c.* 1805 to 1918, and its boys provided guards of honour for visiting minor royalties. There were commercial schools of many varying sizes: Mr. Mason's Commercial School in Winchester (Canon Street) was only very modest; Mr. Walker's College in Portsmouth was larger and numbered amongst its early pupils the future Sir Arthur Conan Doyle. Private schools with good standards had to be prepared to be 'recognised'; that is approved by the State Inspectorate, and the State grammar schools founded under the Act of 1902 charged a small fee, though not to those children who had passed the eleven-plus.

The abolition of school fees in State schools and the raising of the school leaving age have produced many educational changes in Hampshire. Population growths have produced problems too; estimated populations growths, not fulfilled, have produced other difficulties. Changes in government policy have worried some parents and pleased others, and the decision to end grammar schools and selection at 'eleven plus' or at any other age, remains controversial. Hampshire County Council have in fact implemented central government decisions without delay, and comprehensive schools have come into existence all over the county, though Churchers' College at Petersfield and King Edward VI school at Southampton have retained their independence as aided boys' grammar schools. More than half the County Council's annual budget is spent on education, but there are still many needs un-met; there is always a shortage of residential homes for the mentally handicapped, and attempts to provide nursery education had been restricted by the present need for national economies, though some nursery classes have been provided in areas of great social need. There have been tremendous strides in the development of Polytechnics and Colleges of Technology in all the great centres of population, and the long-established Winchester School of Art has been rebuilt and now serves the whole country. John Pound of Portsmouth, the poor cobbler

94

who died in 1839, and who taught his young neighbours to read and write, is a long distance in time from the recent visit of the Hampshire County Youth Orchestra to the United States of America.

One aspect of education to which it seems fitting to draw attention in any account of Hampshire's history is the development of a wide-spread interest in local history and the growth of differing kinds of educational establishments which helped that interest. The Mechanics' Institutes, from their very beginning in 1835 were always interested in the county's history, and instructed their members by buying books, printing pamphlets, and arranging lectures. The first Public Library Act of 1850 made it possible for local authorities to provide libraries and museums. The Hampshire Museum, founded in 1847, and under the inspired direction of Henry Moody, was eventually taken over by the Winchester Council and opened on 10 November 1851 as a museum and a library in the (converted) governor's house of the old county gaol in Jewry Street. It was the first of a series of buildings, constructed for other purposes, re-used to house collections of inestimable educational value. The number includes the Portsmouth Museum and Record Office in the complex of the Clarence Barracks there, and the Hampshire County Record Office splendidly housed in a large redundant Victorian church.

Officers' quarters, Victoria Barracks, Portsmouth

The foundation of the Hampshire Field Club and Archaeological Society by T. W. Shore (1840-1905) with three like minded spirits, in March 1885, was another example of how Hampshire people were becoming interested in Hampshire history. The Hampshire Record Society, active by 1888, was the result of the activities of such local scholars as Dean Kitchin, and the outstanding F. J. Baigent, and of the scholarly collaboration of other editors from the Bodleian Library and the British Museum. Pride in Hampshire's history permeated every corner of society, culminating in the great national pageant of Hampshire's story re-enacted at Wolvesey in 1908, an educational project if ever there was one, and for an international purpose, the restoration of Winchester Cathedral.

XVI Recent Change in Church and State

John Keble

*Memorial to
John Keble*

The Industrial Revolution increased the size of Hampshire's bigger towns, and the coming of the railways in the first half of the 19th century encouraged the growth of new centres of population. Not only had local government to be reformed, but the Anglican Church had to keep up with the times, and eventually the boundaries of the old diocese were re-arranged and new sees created in heavily-populated areas. For 40 years, from 1827, the diocese was under the care of Richard Charles Sumner, a great evangelist, and the first bishop to be installed in person in Winchester Cathedral since the Reformation. His best-known reform was the implementation of a proper scheme for the administration of St. Cross Hospital, which had been the subject of a major scandal, and his clergy included such differing men as John Keble at Hursley and Charles Kingsley at Eversley. Keble, the writer of many famous hymns, was the friend and tutor of Sir William Heathcote of Hursley Park (1801–81), that very prototype of a perfect Victorian squire and English country gentleman, whose circle included the famous novelist, Charlotte Yonge of Otterbourne House, Florence Nightingale and George Moberly, the reforming headmaster of Winchester College. Charles Kingsley, author of *The Water Babies*, was nationally known for his support of social reform; unlike Keble he was a low churchman and a follower of Charles Simeon, whose biographer, Canon Carus, lived in Winchester and created a new parish there—Christ Church, to meet the needs of its growing population.

In 1895, the northern (London) end of the diocese became the independent bishopric of Southwark under E. S. Talbot, a great leader who moved on to become bishop of Winchester in 1911. Cyril Garbett, one of his successors in both Southwark and Winchester, had served as a parish priest in St. Mary's Kingston, near Portsmouth, where he had been outstanding in his realisation that the Anglican Church had a real message for the mass of working-class folk to be found in Hampshire's growing towns. By the time that he became Bishop of Winchester in 1932 the two sees of Guildford and Portsmouth had been created (in 1927), though the present diocese still includes the Channel Islands, annexed to it in 1568, and most of the pre-1972 county of Hampshire including Bournemouth, but not the Isle of Wight, which is under the Bishop of Portsmouth. There has been more recent recognition of the importance of other centres of

96

29. Anthony Henley of Crawley, 1734: MP for Southampton 1727–8.

30. (*below*) Buriton Manor, home of Edmund Gibbon.

31. Hamble: water-colour by G. F. Prosser.

32. (*left*) L. D. G. Tregonwell, 1758–1832. Founder of Bournemouth.

33.   Petersfield in *c*. 1830.

34.   Fareham in *c*. 1830.

COUNTY OF HANTS.

THE EASTERN OR PETERSFIELD DIVISION
PARLIAMENTARY ELECTION
14th JULY, 1892.

OFFICIAL DECLARATION of the POLL

I, HENRY ALFRED JOSEPH DOUGHTY TICHBORNE, BARONET, Sheriff and Returning Officer,

Give Notice, That the total number of Votes given for each Candidate at the above Election is as follows—

WICKHAM,
WILLIAM, of Binsted Wyck, Alton, Hants, Esquire.

3912

BONHAM-CARTER,
JOHN, of Adhurst St. Mary, Petersfield, in the County of Hants, Landowner and Farmer.

3008

Also that the name of the Candidate elected is—

WILLIAM WICKHAM, Esquire.

HENRY ALFRED JOSEPH DOUGHTY TICHBORNE, BARONET,
SHERIFF, and RETURNING OFFICER.

Dated at Petersfield this 15th day of July, 1892.

Printed & Published by John T. Doswell, 1, St. Peter Street, Winchester.

35. The result of the poll, 1892.

36. (*below*) Election propaganda, Bishop's Waltham 1905: 'Cheap Food'.

population in the titles of the suffragan bishops, of Southampton and Basingstoke, the latter a very recent creation. From the mid-19th century onwards, too, there were great changes at parish level. Many new parishes were formed, new churches built, and by 1918 nearly half the parishes in the diocese had been created in the previous one hundred years. Bournemouth, that new town, had 14 parishes, Portsmouth 19 new churches, Southampton 16, and there were others in Aldershot and Eastleigh, as well as in the Botley area, the 'strawberry' churches built in the early stages of a growing population, long before the days of the famous South Hampshire Plan.

Charles Kingsley's grave, Eversley

Since 1945 the situation has changed radically, and though the Anglican Church still has a conscious policy of putting churches where there are people, many parish churches have been closed, declared redundant, pulled down, used for secular purposes, or at best united with neighbouring parishes. Gone are the days when a vacancy for a curate in some well-known parish could produce more than 70 applicants, as was once the case in St. Thomas's church in Winchester. The real shortage of candidates for the ministry is not confined to the Anglican Church, and many a Hampshire town and village now has its share of empty chapels, either through lack of support or because the ecumenical movement has united those who used to be in separate congregations.

Yet much of Hampshire has remained untouched by the Industrial Revolution, and there are still remote villages with historic parish churches greatly loved and admirably maintained by a local population composed largely of commuters travelling daily to Hampshire's large towns or to London. Only a very few small towns and villages can offer a reasonable and varied measure of local employment, and the number of men required for Hampshire's oldest industry, farming, is falling rapidly. The 'journey to work' can be a tiresome problem, though it has to be admitted that some people prefer not to find work on their own doorsteps. Among the smaller towns famous for particular industries, Alton has long been the centre of a great brewery, which has just moved to Reading; Whitchurch and Laverstoke still produce the famous paper for the banknotes of the world: Henri de Portal, a Huguenot refugee, had opened a paper mill at Bere Mill on the Test near Whitchurch in 1712, which proved to be a marvellously successful enterprise. Conder Engineering, which began in Kings Worthy in 1947, had been amongst the most successful of all Hampshire's post-war developments, and become a world-famous name. Other successful family businesses prospered on the coast. In the 18th century famous shipbuilding families included the Adams of Bucklers Hard, who built the *Agamemnon*, the first shop of the line

A prison hulk: H.M.S. York, off Portsmouth

to be commanded by Nelson, whose flagship at Copenhagen was the *Elephant*, built by the firm of Parsons at Bursledon, another small family business. But these small yards which had built wooden ships were soon surpassed by the naval development of Portsmouth, where Victoria opened the Steam Basin in 1848 and where there were extensive extensions of the Dockyard, including the building of dry docks. The Royal Naval Gunnery School, started in 1832 in H.M.S. *Excellent,* was transferred to Whale Island, a site reinforced by convict labour from the prison hulks nearby. The population of Portsea Island, 34,484 in 1811, had virtually doubled by 1851, and by 1901 was 180,000.

The revival of Southampton from the decline noticed by Celia Fiennes and Daniel Defoe was brought about in the first instance by improvements in transport and 18th-century interest in watering places and spas. Sea bathing on the western shore there was tried by the Prince of Wales in 1750, who returned many times, and the place became fashionable. There were further visits from royalties; baths and assembly rooms were created, the Polygon was begun, and the eccentric second Marquis of Lansdowne built himself a Gothic mansion on the site of the Plantagenet Castle. The future of Southampton did not depend, however, on its visitors or on its success as a spa. The rapid commercial development of the port was signalled in 1833 when the Duchess of Kent opened the chain pier; a dock company was incorporated in 1836, and the first dry dock opened in 1846. The completion of the London-Southampton railway line assured Southampton's future as a great commercial port of call for the freighters and increasingly large passenger liners which helped to produce the town's later prosperity. Richard Andrews (d. 1859), a radical politician of very humble origin who had made a fortune, did much for this prosperity by encouraging the interest of wealthy Americans, and Southampton's role as Hampshire's fashionable seaside resort was filled by Bournemouth. George III had visited Mudeford in 1803, and it was from this fashionable village that L. D. G. Tregonwell (1758–1852) drove over to 'Bourne' in 1810 and decided to build himself a home there. The staple industry of that little village had been smuggling, but the building of a family mansion at 'Bourne' by Tregonwell assured the place a wholly respectable future, and soon much of the area was laid out to the design of a fashionable architect from Christchurch, Benjamin Ferrey. The *Bath* hotel, built in 1837, was opened on Victoria's Coronation Day in 1838, and the district became famous not only for its natural advantages of delightful scenery and good climate, but also for its hotels and large private houses. Ferrey's successor, Decimus Burton, suggested that a

Richard Andrews' memorial, Andrews Park, Southampton

98

carriage-bridge be built over the Bourne stream, and one result of this was The Square. Bournemouth's prosperity was assured by the railway, as was the growth of Eastleigh and the establishment of the great military centre at Aldershot in the north of Hampshire, a vast camp built on undeveloped land purchased by the government.

St. Mary's church, Kingston, Portsmouth, c.1850

To some limited extent the brewing of beer took the place formerly held by the cloth industry, and by the middle of the 19th century few towns had much left in the way of the weaving and textile domestic industries which had once produced some measure of local prosperity. Sacks for hops were made at Alton, stockings knitted at Christchurch and Ringwood, and special kinds of silk made at Overton, Whitchurch, and Winchester, but Hampshire's deservedly famous cloths had long disappeared, and the textile industry was established in the north of England. In 1901 less than 50,000 people were employed in Hampshire's shops and factories, and the county was still predominantly agricultural, although there was some talk of prospecting for coal. It was the commercial and naval development of south Hampshire which produced the problems of the century, for the populations of Southampton and Portsmouth continued to grow steadily in the later years of Victoria's reign, and public buildings grew in size and splendour, too, although there was much bad housing and many slums. Some good houses survived, including Charles Dickens' birthplace in Portsmouth. John Wood's County Hospital (1759) in Winchester was replaced by a new building designed by William Butterfield, whose advisers included Sir William Heathcote and Miss Nightingale. Portsmouth's splendid new town hall was designed by William Hill of Leeds in 1886–90; old St. Mary's church at Kingston was replaced by Sir Arthur Blomfield's vast building. The mother church of Southampton, St. Mary's, was rebuilt, too, its spire completed in 1914, in order to cater for the parish's population which had increased nearly 50-fold by the end of the 19th century; Southampton's new Civic Centre, the lineal descendant of the tiny Guildhall over Bargate, was not completed until 1939. Both these coastal towns had major social problems. In Southampton too great a proportion of the population relied on the docks. In Portsmouth, the major employer was the Royal Dockyard. Neither town could find sufficient land to house their growing populations within their own boundaries, and the war of 1939 only increased these difficulties. Homes and jobs were in short supply, and the destruction by bombing of large areas of Portsmouth and Southampton left many families homeless. This real need for new houses coincided with a shortage of traditional building materials, with a system of licensing for all kinds of building, and with the first real Town and Country Planning Act of 1947.

Dickens' birthplace, Portsmouth

Florence Nightingale's church at East Wellow

Moreover, London was thought to be too crowded, and the Town Development Act of 1953 made it possible for local authorities to build houses outside of their own areas, with the result that there were soon suggestions for settling 'overspill' populations in Hampshire towns: Hook, Ringwood, and Winchester were among the possibilities, as well as an entirely new 'Solent City' between Southampton and Portsmouth, for South Hampshire was considered to be a major growth area. Heavy industry was no longer confined to the Royal Naval Dockyard at Portsmouth or to the needs of the Merchant Navy at Southampton, and the construction of a huge oil refinery on Southampton Water seemed to be an indication of South Hampshire's future. The New Forest no longer produces timber for the Royal Navy, but if it is to survive it will have to be vigilantly protected from those who love to visit it, for the tourist industry has become a major factor in Hampshire's modern economy, and it is fortunate that the scheme to expand Ringwood was never implemented. Bournemouth, the Isle of Wight, and Winchester, too, have all become important holiday and tourist centres. Agriculture had declined since the 1880s, but it revived to some extent during the war years of 1939-45. Today there are severe demands on land for building. With the help of a large consultative committee, the South Hampshire Structure Plan was published in 1974 by the Hampshire County Council and submitted to central government, and though a final decision has not yet been reached, it seems certain that 'Solent City' will not be created, and that the growth of Southern Hampshire in terms of population will not be so great as was first expected.

In the north-east of the county work began in 1974 on a similar plan on a sub-regional basis, and covering the area of Reading, Woking, Aldershot and Basingstoke, another potential 'growth area' but Basingstoke, one of Hampshire's typical small market towns, had already been expanded, and the parish church of St. Michael is now dwarfed by skyscraper buildings. Many London firms have opened offices; there are new headquarters for the Civil Service Commissioners and the Automobile Association; and homes have had to be provided for many hundreds of Londoners. There are new schools, and a new shopping centre in the midst of the old town, and there is inevitably much controversy over the appearance of the whole place. Andover is Hampshire's other 'expanded' town. In 1961 the Borough Council there agreed with Hampshire County Council and the Greater London Council that population and industry should be brought from London, and Andover, once a quiet little market town, has today grown beyond recognition and is the largest town in the new District of the Test Valley, with a population of about 27,000. New housing estates have

Basingstoke District coat of arms

100

been constructed on the edges of old Andover, the shopping centre has been rebuilt, though the Market Place has survived with the old Guildhall and the parish church after a good deal of local controversy. A vast new complex, completed in 1975, includes Cricklade College which is a Technical College and a Sixth Form College combined, Magistrates' Courts, and a Sports Centre. There are big industrial estates to the east and west, many new car parks, and an Andover by-pass was opened in 1969, though one of the two railway stations, the line to Southampton, was closed down in 1964.

Modern dripstone, Winchester Cathedral

Winchester's silk mill in St. Peter Street, which moved to large premises in the Abbey Mill in 1793, was an unusual development in a town little changed by the Industrial Revolution and one where change usually meant the development of the traditional industries found in a county town, particularly brewing and printing. There were six printing firms in Winchester in 1859, breweries and malting houses were increasing in number, and manual labour was needed in the leather trades and brickmakers' yards; for the city had outgrown its medieval boundaries, and new buildings were beginning to cover the empty western and eastern downlands which overlooked the ancient town. Churches and the town hall were rebuilt to meet the new needs.

Change of a differing kind has come to Winchester since 1939; it is still the county town of Hampshire, and the diocesan capital, but it finds itself under increasing pressure from office development, and from the many tourists which helped its prosperity. Very few people, less than 1,000, now live within the city centre, and the place has devoured its neighbouring hamlets and villages of St. Cross, Fulflood, Weeke, and Winnall, the last now developed as an industrial estate. The cathedral is no longer the largest building in the city, but is rivalled, if that is the word, by modern offices and car park development. Winchester, in fact, shares the problems of all of Hampshire's smaller historic towns, suffering from the twin pressures of population and the motor car. Old Southampton and old Portsmouth were almost inevitably the casualties of a world war, but it would be a historic disaster if the smaller towns were to become the casualties of peace. There is no doubt that Hampshire, always a county of change, a county made by the passing of time, is changing rapidly in 1976, and that some of this change is too rapid. The land must retain its distinctive character, with its inherent variations, and a knowledge of Hampshire's history helps to secure its future place in the life of the nation.

Farley Mount: memorial to a horse

XVII Local Government in Hampshire, 1066-1976

It seems necessary first to define local government, for in 1976 many matters which appear to be truly local are in fact the concern of central government, and not the responsibility of local authorities elected by the local electorate.

Local government is government of a particular geographical area by an individual or group of individuals, whose authority is derived from central government. The strength of Norman administration in Hampshire depended basically on the efficiency of the Sheriff, the king's local representative in the county, but the county had had at least one Anglo-Saxon Sheriff, Ezi, who owned land at Tatchbury in the parish of Eling, and a small estate in Barton Stacey which eventually passed to his Norman successor, Hugh de Port. Ezi's main duty must have been to preside over the shire court where the principal suitors were Hampshire thegns, and the main business the ownership of land. Below the shire court, the administrative unit of law and order was the Hundred, which remained a nominal division of the county until the present century. The names of the Hampshire Hundreds are not always easy to explain, but the division itself is very ancient and goes back at least to the time of King Edgar. His ordinance of the Hundred required the Hundred courts to meet every four weeks and justice to be done to all. Each Hundred was further divided into Tythings, perhaps in origin a group of 10 families, and the tything man was responsible for the arrest of criminals in his area. When Anglo-Saxon kings were in Hampshire and assembled the Witenagemot to advise them, influential local men were summoned to attend; but local government in Hampshire before 1066 showed little sign of democracy, though there were ancient assemblies, usually held out of doors, on a natural hill, beneath a well-known tree, or in pagan times at the burial places of a well-known chieftain. After the conversion the great preaching crosses were obvious assembly points, and it is tempting to suggest that solution as the explanation of the widening of Winchester's High Street at the High Cross. Southampton met at Cuttmorn, and in the New Forest the Moot House at Downton provides another example, in its garden, of a site which must have seen some important meetings.

The Normans imposed their own forms of bureaucracy on the Anglo-Saxon structure which they found, and the Sheriffs became

102

very powerful indeed. They received the royal commands in the form of writs, receipts which directed that certain actions be taken, and if necessary used their armed forces or *posse* to enforce that action. They made the arrangements in Winchester for holding the Assize, the sittings of the King's Justices on circuit; and the Sheriff was always a member of the Assize Commission, which inevitably included a number of local magnates and important ecclesiastics.

It was the Sheriff's duty, too, to act as the king's financial officer in Hampshire, to collect the royal revenue, including the farms of towns, and also to pay out monies on the king's behalf. The Sheriff's accounts had to be audited twice in a year at Easter and Michaelmas at the Exchequer in Westminster Palace, and they were written up in a great formal record known as the Pipe Roll. The earliest surviving roll dates from 1130, though the series is only more or less complete from the reign of Henry II, and the Pipe Rolls are a primary source for the history of local government and its finance, for they show how money flowed from the county into the royal purse. The section of the roll dealing with Hampshire bears the name of the county, and usually has certain well-defined divisions, and Hampshire Sheriffs were usually county gentlemen, professional civil servants. Sir Simon de Winton, Sheriff in 1283, who had previously been mayor of Winchester, had property in many parts of the county—Fulflood, Lainston, Otterbourne and Soberton—and was very wealthy, but neither he nor the majority of other Sheriffs can be described as great feudal magnates. Accumulated moneys were left in Winchester Castle in the royal treasury, and although this was moved to Westminster at the end of the 12th century, very large sums were still left in Winchester for the next 100 years: in 1208 nearly six and a half million pennies had to be counted in the Winchester treasury.

The power of the Sheriff, in reality so dependent on the king, was challenged eventually, and successfully, by the larger Hampshire towns; but in the countryside, the growth of local independence was very slow, and the old Anglo-Saxon courts declined. On some manors where the medieval peasant was brave enough to try to insist on his manorial rights, manorial courts could be used to uphold the ancient custom and therefore the ancient rights and privileges of the lord's tenants. There is plenty of evidence in Domesday to suggest that even a small community could speak its own mind, particularly in matters of taxation. Royal Meon, worth £60, pays £100, 'but it is not able to bear it'. Bishop's Meon pays £40, but it is worth only £30, and five royal manors in the Isle of Wight paid £77 instead of their rightful £50. In the late 13th century even an important man like Sir Simon de Winton was called to the Assize to show why he had wrongfully assessed his tenants in Otterbourne; and at Crondall in 1364, where the manor belonged to St. Swithun's Priory, the tenants complained to the king about additional services and rents demanded from them.

By that time central government was in grave financial difficulties; Edward I's military expeditions were particularly expensive, and neither he nor his successors cared sufficiently for the county to produce enough money to repair the royal apartments in Winchester Castle, burnt out in a disastrous fire in 1302. William of Wykeham was blamed for the financial disaster of the Hundred Years War, and Richard II's notorious poll tax of November 1380, a levy of three groats on everyone over 15 years of age, added to the general discontent throughout Hampshire and apparently precipitated a rising against the oligarchy in Winchester. Henry V's French expeditions increased the Crown's debts, and produced only a measure of temporary war-time prosperity in the ports and in Winchester. All these national difficulties, combined with the decline in population after the Black Death, produced many financial problems and much social unrest. Attempts to fix wages by Statute and to control the movement of labour were entrusted to Hampshire men appointed from 1360 onwards to the new office of Justice of the Peace. In general terms, it can be said that for the next 500 years what local government there was in the Hampshire countryside was the work of these unpaid magistrates, the maids-of-all-work of central government.

The Reformation and the end of monasticism meant that the task of relieving the poor and needy was placed on the only form of organisation readily available, the parish. The Beggars' Act of 1536 required parishes to appoint officers to raise and distribute alms, County Justices set up a workhouse in the course of 1576, and the great Poor Relief Act of 1601 became a permanent feature of local government; every parish had to 'set the poor on work', under the supervision of the Justices of the Peace. Evasions or arguments between parishes had to be dealt with by magistrates meeting in Quarter Sessions, usually held in some comfortable inn or in a private house, and most Justices were honest, respectable and influential members of the community. It was unfortunate that the political troubles of the 17th century prevented the Hampshire county bench from achieving any measure of impartiality; towns which had their own Commission of the Peace, like Winchester and Southampton, produced other problems, for many town J.P.'s were also members of their local Corporations, and this absence of the separation of powers was unfortunate. Most Justices in fact were unpopular, and the Bench gained the reputation of being 'against the working classes'.

Magistrates, too, had to oversee the spending of money raised by

104

37. Basingstoke, *c.* 1831, with the windmill erected in 1822, and Warwick, a famous dray horse.

38. Southampton, *c.* 1840.

PORTSMOUTH FAIR.

39. Portsmouth Fair.

40. (*above*) The West Gate, Winchester, *c.* 1874.

41. South side, Winchester High Street, after renovation.

42.   The late Miss Beatrice Forder rebinding the Winchester Bible in the Morley Library.

43.   Diocesan Training College, 1862. (John Colson, Architect)

rates for the repair and maintenance of roads and bridges. A parish with a bridge to maintain which served the county as a whole could only hope to get it taken over as a county responsibility—like the bridge over the Test at Romsey, accepted by the County Magistrates in 1607, and the bridge at Stockbridge in 1639; Redbridge was a very expensive bridge to keep up, because it spanned a tidal river and was frequently damaged. Parishioners whose local roads were also main Hampshire highways were as unfortunate as those with county bridges; Compton was virtually cut in half by the main Southampton–Winchester road, and arguments about the upkeep had to go to Quarter Sessions. The other work of the Hampshire Bench included the upkeep of the County Hall, used for many different trials, including those of Sir Walter Raleigh in 1603, and Alicia Lisle in 1685; it was a notoriously difficult building in terms of acoustics, but its brutal partitioning by order of Quarter Sessions in 1764 did not add to its aesthetic appearance. Hampshire owes its splendid renovation in 1871 to Melville Portal, then the chairman of Hampshire Quarter Sessions. Since that date it has again suffered partitioning, but the abolition of Assizes and the opening of the new Crown Courts in Winchester in 1974 has made possible a further restoration.

Prisoners tried in the Hall by County Justices or Assize Judges had to be kept in safe custody or were sometimes returned to imprisonment. There were many differing prisons in medieval Hampshire, in Carisbrooke Castle, at Lyndhurst, Odiham, Portchester, Portsmouth, and Southampton, but the county gaol was in Winchester, and its nominal keeper held by serjeantry the manor of Woodcote in Bramdean. In reality, the Sheriff dealt with most prison matters. Later on, Quarter Sessions were responsible for the maintenance of the County Prison, on a site in Winchester in Staple Gardens and Jewry Street since the 12th century. In the early 19th century George Moneypenny, the architect, was commissioned to design a debtors' prison on its Jewry Street frontage, and remnants of this frontage still remain, but the building was eventually replaced in 1847 by a new prison on the Romsey Road, designed by Thomas Stopher, senior, another well-known architect. This is the prison still in use, made famous for all time in the last pages of *Tess of the D'Urbervilles*.

All this important work, work of local government, was carried on by the unpaid magistrates, with the help of a few permanent officials headed by the Clerk of the Peace, always a lawyer, whose income came from fees and not a salary. There were two nominal Treasurers, Magistrates, for all the funds; but real financial administration was in the hands of a number of paid deputies for specified matters, and when one man was deputy for more than one fund, the work of his present

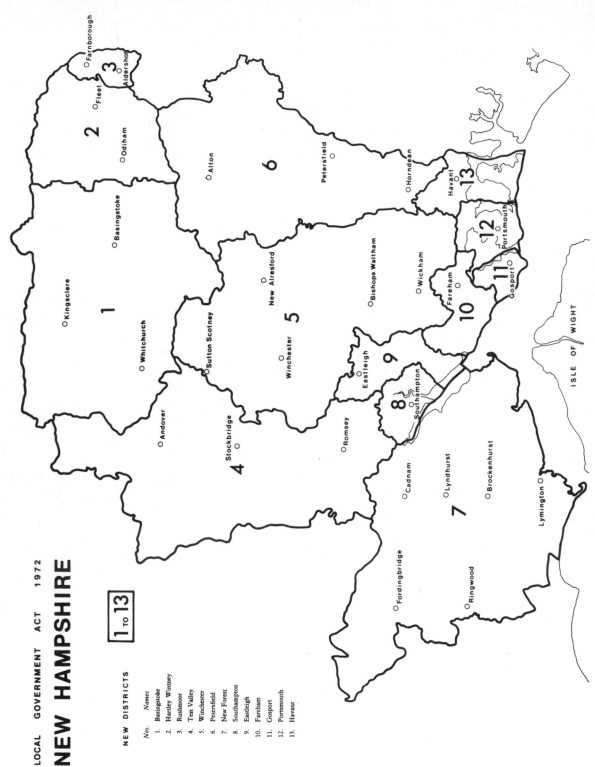

LOCAL GOVERNMENT ACT 1972

NEW HAMPSHIRE

1 to 13

NEW DISTRICTS

Nos.	Names
1.	Basingstoke
2.	Hartley Wintney
3.	Rushmoor
4.	Test Valley
5.	Winchester
6.	Petersfield
7.	New Forest
8.	Southampton
9.	Eastleigh
10.	Fareham
11.	Gosport
12.	Portsmouth
13.	Havant

Farnborough

Fleet

Aldershot

3

2

Odiham

Alton

6

Petersfield

Horndean

Havant

13

Basingstoke

12

Portsmouth

Kingsclere

1

New Alresford

Bishops Waltham

Wickham

Fareham

11

Gosport

Whitchurch

Sutton Scotney

5

10

Winchester

Eastleigh

9

Andover

Stockbridge

4

Romsey

Southampton

8

ISLE OF WIGHT

Cadnam

Lyndhurst

Brockenhurst

7

Lymington

Fordingbridge

Ringwood

Map 13. Hampshire re-organised.

successor, the present-day County Treasurer, had begun. It is not surprising, however, that by the end of the 18th century there were thoughtful people in Hampshire who questioned a system of local government by magistrates who were not elected, and who were spending large sums of public money raised by rates. William Cobbett, the radical politician, detested the High Tory Justices of the county; and even reformers who were less extreme than that farmer from Botley thought that some sort of change must come, and that Hampshire ought to be governed by men who had been elected for the task. The alternatives seemed too dreadful to contemplate: many Hampshire gentlemen had signed the petition 'against' the French Revolution in 1793, and the *Hampshire Chronicle*, aghast at the violence in France, became a High Tory paper. In Southampton there

A prisoner's drawing

was so much fear of reform that what has been called 'an alliance for the defence of Society' came into existence. In 1830, the riots of Hampshire's agricultural workers were among the most serious in the countryside, and there were serious disturbances at Barton Stacey, Holybourne, Hawkley and Selborne; Sir William Heathcote at Hursley strengthened his house with iron shutters, and there were too many prisoners for the county gaol. The year 1830 probably strengthened the minds of those who believed that the countryside was not yet ready for democracy, and even the great Parliamentary Reform Act of 1832 and the reform of the Municipal Corporations in 1835 did not end corruption, nor violence at election time in Hampshire towns, though Stockbridge lost its members of parliament. A list of all electors entitled to vote in every borough in local elections had to be published; the surviving freemen, until they died out, were allowed to vote in all towns and the practice was extended to all resident males over the age of 21 except for the very poorest. The old system had become deplorable: in Portsmouth, with a population of 46,000, the right to vote had been restricted to some 102 persons. Town councils now had to be directly elected for a varied number of wards, councillors served for three years, and there were to be a small number of aldermen (serving six years) elected by the council with the object of providing some continuity. Voting, however, was still open, and lists published after each election showed how votes were cast. Intimidation was possible and not infrequent; noisy and sometimes violent crowds of young men, not able to vote, were active in elections. Moreover, the new councils did not always interest the most able men in the community, who shrank from the rough-and-tumble of a local election; there were too many small local tradesmen on all the new councils, whose interest in rates was wholly negative. Fear of putting up the rates delayed main sewerage in Winchester for over 30 years.

Between 1835 and the Local Government Reform Act of 1888 which set up county councils, something like chaos grew up in local government; local work of all kinds was committed to different kinds of boards. The old Poor Law had been reformed in 1834, and parishes grouped into unions. The old Hundreds may have been the basis of the new union in some counties, but this does not appear to have been the case in Hampshire. Soon a whole variety of Boards were in operation levying rates, and maintaining large staffs of officers: their members in Hampshire were being elected at widely differing times of the year with differing franchises. A Hampshire elector in 1885 in town and county might have to vote, in the same year, for Town Councils, Boards of Guardians of the Poor, Highway Boards, School Boards Lighting Inspectors, and Burial Boards, to mention only a few examples. There was no system; differing boards administered differing work all over the county—in fact, all over England.

Reform in local government came at last in 1888, with a Local Government Act dealing with county government. County Councils were set up, with three-quarters of their members elected direct, the rest being aldermen chosen by the other members. When the first election took place in Hampshire, most of those chosen proved to be county magistrates, and the work of local government was carried on in much the same way as before, although the Great Hall on the Western Hill, with the magistrates' offices, proved wholly inadequate for the staff of the new authority. Massive extensions of county council offices building became a feature of Winchester's landscape. The same Reform Act (of 1888) allowed the great towns, Portsmouth, Southampton and eventually Bournemouth, to become county boroughs, virtually independent of the County Council and 'trading' direct with central government; their status was determined by the size of their population, fixed at 50,000 in 1888. Attempts to include the Isle of Wight in the new Hampshire County Council were not successful, and a measure of independence at local level was made possible by the Parish Council Acts of 1894, which also created Urban and District Councils in areas of Hampshire where there was no one specific growing area of population. The boundaries of these new 'U.D.C.s' and 'R.D.C.s' were those of the old Sanitary Boards.

Before 1972 there was much variety of local government in Hampshire, and Eastleigh provides a good example of how much change there could be. The coming of the London–Southampton railway in 1840 transformed an area which was wholly rural, that of the ancient manor of Eastleigh and the ancient parish of Bishopstoke. By 1864 Thomas Chamberlayne had acquired the manor, and began to grant building leases, and in the late 1880s the London and South Western

Hampshire County Badge, adopted 1895

108

Railway Company moved their carriage and wagon works from Nine Elms to Basingstoke. A place which had started as a village of some 300 houses became an Urban District of 6,000 people, was extended in 1888/9 to include North and South Stoneham and Bishopstoke, and became a borough by royal charter in 1936.

The war of 1939–45 put a temporary stop to talk of further change in local government, but after it was over the debate was renewed. There were those who thought that the County Council should be abolished, and that Hampshire should be divided into uniform areas each virtually independent of each other, able to communicate with central government direct. There were others who considered that the very foundations of democracy needed strengthening, that parish councils should be given more powers, and that a County Council with certain overall powers might prevent local mistakes, particularly in the fields of planning. Not everybody was very impressed by the new Basingstoke, new Andover, or the rebuilding of central Portsmouth and Southampton.

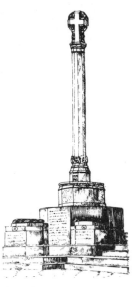

The County War Memorial

The Local Government Act of 1972 set up a two-tiered system of local government in Hampshire of County Council and new District Councils. The status of all the long-established boroughs, cities, and county-boroughs, and the more recent Urban and Rural District Councils, was abolished. Hampshire boundaries were affected, including Bournemouth and Christchurch, which disappeared into Dorset, and the geographical area that remained was divided up into 13 District Councils, each with its own elected government. Of these new Councils, three, Portsmouth, Southampton, and Gosport, retained the boundaries of the pre-1972 towns. Other District Councils, Basingstoke, Eastleigh, Havant, Fareham, and Winchester, were based on a town nucleus of the same name; in the New Forest, the district is what its name implies and includes the ancient borough of Lymington. A stranger to the county might be permitted some feeling of uncertainty about the boundaries of the other District Councils, Hart, East Hampshire, Rushmoor, and the Test Valley, though these were names chosen after much careful thought. In this new two-tiered local government the old County Council's situation was greatly strengthened: former county boroughs, great cities like Portsmouth and Southampton, can no longer control their own educational or highway policies, and, a sore point in a city like Winchester, local libraries are also managed by the county. The Act envisaged the making of agency arrangements for some of these matters, and to some extent the success of the reform in terms of relationship between County Council and District Councils will depend on the success of these agency arrangements. One important result of the first County Council election after

Southampton, Terminus Station, 1839–40

109

*Police superintend-
ent's cart, c.1900*

the Act was that the County Council has become very political, and the old system of county aldermen was abolished. Aldermen were abolished, too, in the new District Councils, where the new authorities were now required to sever some of their historical connections if they so wished and elect to be ruled by a district chairman instead of a mayor. Districts which have taken the other option, Gosport, Portsmouth, Southampton, Eastleigh, Havant, and Winchester, have district mayors. Small towns lying within Districts which have chairmen are permitted to have town mayors, but the options have produced difficulties. It is easy to understand why the survival of an ancient mayoralty can be troublesome to a District Council, even though town mayors have few real powers, and conversely it is historically difficult to imagine Winchester in particular without its mayoralty, the oldest in Hampshire, and the second oldest in the kingdom.

There are other features of the reform of 1972 which have produced difficulties of administration, and sometimes clashes of personalities. The new councils which contain a large number of civil parishes taken in from old urban or rural district councils are obliged to consult parish councils on a number of important matters, including planning applications, though the parish is not able to determine applications. Finance is a particular problem: a specific purpose of the Act was to end differential rating, the old system by which countrymen paid less than townsmen on the grounds that the townsmen had more amenities. A large proportion of the total rate is levied by the County Council, though collected by the Districts, and used throughout the county for Hampshire matters—education and roads, to name only two of the biggest spenders. Education consumes half the county's budget. Rural users still have some slight financial advantage in differential rating, but the gap will soon disappear. It is unfortunate that Local Government Reform was rushed through parliament in 1972 without any real consideration of the needs of local government finance, which will have to be one day the subject of further reform, perhaps the creation of a separate local income tax. Another difficult matter in terms of finance has proved to be the Act which created new Water Authorities, removed the supplying of water from local authorities, and created new large water undertakings. Most of Hampshire's water supply is administered by the Southern Water Authority, with a headquarters in Worthing.

Today, more than half of Hampshire's total population lives in the south of the county, in the districts of Southampton, Eastleigh, Fareham, Gosport, Portsmouth, and Havant. In 1974 the total population was 1,434,000 people, and if the national fall in the birth rate continues it is difficult to imagine, as used to be suggested, a dramatic increase on a vast scale in the 1980s, though the work of the County Council will continue to be large-scale. In 1976 there were 97 elected members who served on various committees and employed 55,000 people, dealing with Education (including Youth Employment), Planning and Highways, Social Services, Fire Services, Consumer Protection, Refuse Disposal, and Recreation, which includes libraries and museums. One important committee deals with the Hampshire and Isle of Wight Constabulary, for the County Council is obliged to find money for the Police Force, and 'Social Services' work in close co-operation with the Health Service, the Protection Services and the Police Force. There are few aspects of life, in fact, which are not the concern of the County Council. Historians should not predict the future, but it seems likely that the place of the County Council within an area wider than Hampshire is bound to be discussed if there are realistic proposals for devolution of some central government powers to regional authorities.

Appendix

Some Hampshire histories and brief notes on sources for local history kept within the county in 1976 in Record Offices, museums and Local History Societies.

1. *Early county histories.* The medieval historians of Hampshire were monks, and this tradition was carried into the 15th century by Thomas Rudborne (fl. 1460), a monk of Winchester Cathedral, and the author of several unpublished manuscripts now in the British Museum. After the Reformation it was not always safe to write about contemporary history: Richard White of Basingstoke (1539–1611), a Roman Catholic and an exile from England, wrote a history of England before the Norman Conquest which contains much about King Arthur, an interest continued by other Tudor historians, including the famous topographer-antiquarian John Leland (1605?–1552): the Winchester section of his *Itinerary* was published by Henry Moody, the first curator of Winchester Museum, in his *Notes and Essays on Hampshire and Wiltshire* (Warren, Winchester, 1851), and the Hampshire notes were edited by him in 1868. John Norden (1548–*c.* 1628) was the first topographer-historian to consider the idea of a complete history of England in counties and his (largely unpublished) 'Chronological Description of several Shires' (B.M. Add. MS. 31853) includes Hampshire, but he is probably better known for the splendid Hampshire map drawn for Camden's *Britannia* in 1607, and preceded by Christopher Saxton's map of Hampshire published in 1579, which does not show roads, though it includes bridges. By the time of Herman Moll's map (1742) there were 17 main routes in the county, of which 10 passed through Winchester.

Some historians were particularly interested in the ecclesiastical history of Hampshire. The three great volumes of Sir William Dugdale's *Monasticon* (1655, 1661 and 1673) contain the earliest extant drawings of Hampshire's religious houses, with an accompanying text derived from original materials, including a great number of charters copied and edited from original sources. Henry Wharton, a short-lived young scholar of immense energy and ability, published *Anglia Sacra* in two volumes in 1619, a marvellous collection of original material, including much relating to the diocese of Winchester.

The most notable 17th-century collectors of historical material in Hampshire and the Isle of Wight were a Winchester lawyer, John

Trussell (d. 1648) John Chase, clerk to the Dean and Chapter (d. 1658), and Sir John Oglander of Nunwell. Trussell catalogued his city's muniments, wrote Winchester's history, and continued the *Collection of English History* made by the Elizabethan poet and historian, Samuel Daniel (1562-1619). Chase compiled a real record of the Cathedral's archives and restored them as best he could after they had been ransacked in the Civil War. Hampshire historians owe him a tremendous debt. In the Island, the old Royalist, Oglander, was writing down what he knew about Hampshire and Island families, and his memoranda books, still largely unpublished, are available on microfilm (H.C.R.O. and I.o.W. C.R.O.).

In happier times 100 years later, Dr. John Speed completed the first history of Southampton (1770: published Southampton Record Society, 1909), and another famous town history was that of Winchester, published in 1798 and compiled by the Roman Catholic bishop, John Milner. He was a contemporary of a more professional historian with wider Hampshire interests, Richard Warner of Sway in the New Forest, who edited the Hampshire section of Domesday Book in 1789, and whose *Collections for the History of Hampshire and the Bishopric of Winchester* was apparently published in 1795, without his consent; whoever perpetuated this alleged piracy still did a great service to local history. In 1840 Robert Mudie brought out his *Hampshire,* in three volumes, including the Isle of Wight, charmingly illustrated by a series of illuminating drawings, and the whole technique of historical writing received a further stimulus in the 1850s when the Rev. D. D. Woodward (1816-1869), with T. C. Wilks and C. Lockart, published a magnificent, undated, three-volume *History of Hampshire.* Woodward became Queen Victoria's librarian at Windsor Castle, and his work on Hampshire did much to prepare the way for the five volumes named in honour of the Queen, the *Victoria County History of Hampshire,* published between 1900 and 1914.

2. All the early writers have their own particular value, and it would be foolish to under-rate their importance, despite the fact that the amount of original material available to them was comparatively limited. Today, the would-be writer of local history is faced with a vast mass of local material kept in Record Offices, in museums, and in private collections all over the county. The notes which follow are intended to indicate the main sources of material *kept in Hampshire.*

(A) *City Record Offices*

The three cities of Winchester, Portsmouth and Southampton have had record offices for many years (N.B.: the cities became District

Councils in 1972). They own major collections of original documents, containing *inter alia,* for their particular area:

i. The official records of local government, Winchester from 1155, Portsmouth since 1313, Southampton since 1199.

ii. Personal papers and business records.

iii. Church records of various kinds.

iv. Records of institutions and public undertakings, for example, schools, water-supplies, public transport.

v. Title deeds, Acts of Parliament, including enclosure awards.

Addresses: *Winchester City Record Office,* St. Thomas Church, Southgate Street, Winchester. (Archivist: A. P. Whitaker, M.A.).
(A separate collection, but generously housed within the County Record Office building.)

Southampton Record Office, The Civic Centre, Southampton. (Archivist: Miss S. Thompson, M.A.). *Guide* (published 1964.)

Portsmouth, City Records Officer, W. Nigel Yates, M.A., F.R. Hist. S.
(a) City Record Office, 3 Museums Road, Portsmouth, PO1 2LE.
(b) Guildhall Record Office, Guildhall, Portsmouth, for church records, *including those of the Diocese of Portsmouth.*

(B) *Archive Collections belonging to Ancient Chartered Towns*

i. *Andover:* Access through application to Clerk of the Charter Trustees, Mayor's Parlour, Andover.

ii. *Basingstoke:* c/o County Archivist.

iii. *Romsey:* Access through Clerk of the Council, Town Hall, Romsey.

iv. *Lymington:* Access through Clerk of the Council, Town Hall, Lymington.

v. *Christchurch:* Access through Chief Executing Officer, Town Hall, Christchurch, Dorset.

(C) *The Hampshire County Record Office*

Contains the largest collection of documents in the county, including:

115

i. Personal papers, title deeds, manorial rolls and documents of many landowners.

ii. Probate records, including Wills. (Wills of individuals whose property extended to more than one parish had to be proved in the Probate Court of the Archbishop of Canterbury: these P.C.C. Wills are now in the Public Record Office, Chancery Lane, London.)

iii. Records of local government and public institutions (many maps).

iv. The records of the diocese of Winchester, including parish registers.

Addresses: *The Hampshire County Record Office,* St. Thomas Church, Southgate Street, Winchester. (Archivist: Miss M. Cash, M.A.).

The Diocesan Record Office, St. Thomas Church, Southgate Street, Winchester. (Archivist: Miss M. Cash, M.A.).

The H.C.R.O. contains many useful catalogues to its collections, indices of personal and place names and a supporting library (The Moens Collection) of Hampshire books. Materials relating to *Christchurch* and *Bournemouth* areas (in Dorset since 1974), remain in H.C.R.O.

MUSEUMS IN HAMPSHIRE

Museums Maintained by Local Authorities

There is no central County Museum as such, but there is a:

Hampshire County Museum Service

(Director: K. J. Barton, M.Phil., F.S.A., F.M.A., Chilcomb House, Chilcomb Lane, Bar End, Winchester, SO23 8RD. *Tel.:* 66242-3.)

The service maintains and staffs three small museums and art galleries:

i. *Curtis Museum and Allen Gallery,* Alton. (High Street, Alton, Hants.).

ii. *Willis Museum and Art Gallery,* Basingstoke. (New Street, Basingstoke, Hants.).

iii. *Red House Museum and Art Gallery,* Christchurch Quay Road, Christchurch, Dorset.

There is an information retrieval system for the collections, a file system for every town and village, a good collection of photographs both old and contemporary, and a museum library. All are available for study upon written application to the Director.

The oldest established museum maintained by a local authority is the

Winchester City Museum, founded in 1851. (The Square, Winchester.) (Archaeology, history of Winchester and central Hampshire.)

The Westgate Museum. (Local history, weights and measures, armour.)

The Guildhall Art Gallery. (Broadway, Winchester.)

The former County Boroughs all have large museums:

Portsmouth:

City Museum and Art Gallery, Museum Road, Portsmouth.
Southsea Castle Museum.

Cumberland House Museum, Eastney.

Southampton (all housed in historic buildings):

God's House Tower, Winkle Street, Southampton. (Archaeology; ceramics.)

Tudor House, Bugle Street, Southampton. (Period furniture, costumes.)

Wool House, Bugle Street. (Maritime history.)

Bargate Guildhall, High Street. (Local history.)

Bournemouth (since 1972 in the County of Dorset):

Russell-Cotes Art Gallery and Museum, East Cliff, Bournemouth.

Rothesay Museum, 8 Bath Road, Bournemouth. (Collection includes Victoriana, armour, local natural history.)

Museums illustrating the lives of famous individuals:

Gilbert White Museum and Oates Memorial Library, The Wakes, Selborne, near Alton.

Jane Austen's Home, Chawton, near Alton.

Carisbrooke Castle Museum (in the care of the Department of the Environment), Newport, Isle of Wight. (Archaeology, history, and personal relics of Charles I.)

Charles Dickens' Birthplace Museum, 393 Commercial Road, Portsmouth.

117

St. Michael's Abbey, Farnborough, Hants. (Tombs and relics of Napoleon III and Empress Eugenie.)

Museums concerned with the history of the armed forces:

H.M.S. 'Victory' and Victory Museum, H.M. Dockyard, Portsmouth.

Royal Corps of Transport Model Room and Museum, Longmoor Camp, Liss, Hants. (Limited hours of opening: usually by appointment.

Q.A.R.A.N.C. Museum, The Royal Pavilion, Aldershot. (Army nursing from Crimea to 1976.)

Royal Greenjackets Museum, Peninsula Barracks, Romsey Road, Winchester.

Royal Hampshire Regiment Museum, Serle's House, Southgate Street, Winchester.

Royal Marine Museum, Royal Marine Barracks, Eastney, Southsea.

Submarine Museum, H.M.S. *Dolphin,* Gosport, Hants.

Army Physical Training Corps Museum, Queen's Avenue, Aldershot. Hants. (Period uniforms, equipment, weapons.)

Buckler's Hard Maritime Museum, Buckler's Hard, Hants.

Royal Army Medical Corps, Historical Museum, Keogh Barracks, Ash Vale, Aldershot, Hants.

Small museums, including those at important archaeological sites, or in interesting buildings include—

Calleva Museum, Silchester, Hants. (N.B.: Many of the most important *Calleva* finds are in Reading Museum, Reading, Berks.)

King John's Hunting Box, Romsey, Hants.

God-be-Got House, High Street, Winchester.

Iron Age Farm, Queen Elizabeth II Park, Butser Hill, Petersfield.

Museum-type displays at:

Danebury.

Basing House.

Queen Elizabeth II Park, Butser Hill.

Some Local History Societies

The established county society is:

The Hampshire Field Club and Archaeological Society, Hon. Secretary: Miss E. Lewis, M.A., The Museum, The Square, Winchester.

Societies interested in particular villages or subjects include:

Alresford Historical and Literary Society, Hon. Secretary: J. Adams, Esq., 'Montello', Jacklyne Lane, Alresford, Hants.

Andover Archives Committee, J. Spaul, Esq., 'Cypress Cottage', Longparish, near Andover.

Jane Austen Society, President: Sir Hugh Smiley, 'Ivalls, Alton.

Bishop's Waltham Local History Society, Hon. Secretary: B. Tremlett, Esq., Plot 21, Eastways, Bishop's Waltham.

Botley and Curdridge Local History Society, Hon. Secretary: T. Bishop, Esq., 18 Mortimer Road, Botley.

The William Cobbett Society, Hon. Secretary: J. Grey, Esq., 14 Arle Close, Alresford.

Eastleigh Local History Society, Hon. Secretary: J. Taylor, 4 Romsey Close, Eastleigh.

Fareham Local History Society, Hon. Secretary: Mrs. A. James, 'Woodland Lodge', Wickham, Hants.

Farnham Museum Society, Hon. Secretary: R. C. Powell, Esq., 'Woodbury', Vicarage Lane, The Bourne, Farnham, Surrey.

Hampshire Genealogical Society, Secretary: Mrs. E. Edwards, 21 Lodge Avenue, East Cosham, PO6 2JR.

Petersfield Area Historical Society, Secretary: Miss D. Hex, 10 Castle Gardens, Swan Street, Petersfield.

Friends of Portsmouth City Record Office, Hon. Secretary: Mrs. T. Merewood, 28 Selsey Avenue, Southsea.

Romsey and District Society, Chairman: Dr. J. White, 'Wykeham House', The Hundred, Romsey.

Friends of Old Southampton, Hon. Secretary: T. J. W. de Grouchy, Esq., 1 Khartoum Road, Highfield, Southampton.

Wickham Local History Society, Hon. Secretary: Mrs. K. Blake, 'The Gables', Wickham.

Willis Historical Society, Hon. Secretary, Mrs. B. J. M. Herrington, 16 Scotney Road, Basingstoke, Hants.

Local Societies interested in archaeology and the work of museums include:

Test Valley Archaeological Committee, Hon Secretary: Mrs. P. Berrow, The Old Fire Station, Latimer Street, Romsey.

Lower Test Valley Archaeological Society, Hon. Secretary: Mrs. O. Sherratt, 8 St. Clement's Close, Romsey.

Andover Archaeological Society, Secretary: R. Warmington, Esq., 10 Western Avenue, Andover.

Basingstoke Archaeological Society, c/o The District Council Offices, Basingstoke.

Portsmouth Museums Society, c/o The Curator, Portsmouth Museum, Museums Road, Southsea.

Southampton City Museum Archaeological Society, c/o The Keeper of Archaeology and Antiquities, The Museum, Winkle Street, Southampton.

For aspects of Winchester, *The Winchester Research Unit,* 13 Parchment Street, Winchester, Director: Prof. M. Biddle.

Select Bibliography

The Hampshire Record Society ceased its publications in 1899, but the Hampshire Record Office has just (1976) announced a new series of *Hampshire Records*, beginning with the notebook of *Sir Henry Whitehead*. Other original material is published regularly in *The Southampton Record Series*, by the *Andover* Archives Committee, and in the *Portsmouth Papers*.

Some very important Diocesan records, belonging to the see of Winchester have been listed and published privately by Mr. A. J. Willis. They include Settlement papers, Consistory Court proceedings, lists of Wills, and Marriage licences.

There is no modern Hampshire Bibliography, but three 19th-century bibliographies have recently been re-published in one volume, *Hampshire Bibliographies*, Shurlock (1975).

Southampton's History, A Guide to the printed sources, Southampton Public Libraries (1968), is a valuable town bibliography.

Members of Parliament for Andover, 1295-1885. R. Arnold Jones. Andover Archives Local Committee, 1972.

The Episcopal Colleagues of Thomas Becket (including Henry de Blois). David Knowles. C.U.P., 1951.

William of Wykeham. Robert Lowth. Clarendon Press, 3rd edition, 1777.

William of Wykeham as Patron of the Arts. William Hayter. Chatto and Windus, 1972.

Lives of the Bishops of Winchester (2 vols.). S. H. Cassan. Rivington and Co., 1827.

Lancelot Andrews. Paul A. Welsby. S.P.C.K., 1964.

Roundhead General, Sir William Waller. John Adair. Mcdonald, 1967.

Jane Austen. Elizabeth Jenkins. Gollancz, 1968.

Rodney. David Spinney. George Allen and Unwin, 1969.

Sir William Heathcote. F. Awdry. Wykeham Press, 1905.

Charlotte Mary Yonge. Georgina Battiscombe. Constable and Co., 1943.

William Cobbett. G. D. H. Cole. Home and Van Thal, 1947.

The Dust of Combat: Charles Kingsley. Robert Martin. Faber and Faber, 1959.

Florence Nightingale. C. Woodham Smith. Penguin edition, 1955.

The Tichborne Claimant. Douglas Woodruff. Hollis and Carter, 1957.

Thomas Brassey, Railway Builder. Charles Walker. Methuen, 1969.

Said and Done (an Autobiography). O. G. S. Crawford, 1955.

The House of Commons, 1715-1754. Romney Sedgewick. (History of Parliament Trust). H.M.S.O. 1970.

The House of Commons, 1754-1790. Sir Lewis Namier, John Brooke. (History of Parliament Trust). H.M.S.O. 1964.

The Victoria County History of Hampshire, 5 vols. and index, 1900-1911.

Hampshire in the British Iron Age: Essays in Honour of Frank Warren. C. F. C. Hawkes. H.F.C., Vol. XX, 1956.

St. Catherine's Hill: H.F.C. *Proceedings,* Vol. XI (1930). C. F. C. Hawkes, J. N. L. Myres, C. G. Stevens.

Iron Age Sites in Central Southern England. Barry Cunliffe. C.B.A. Research Report No. 16, 1976.

Danebury, the story of a Hampshire Hill Fort. Barry Cunliffe. Open University Press, 1976.

The Archaeology of Wessex. L. V. Grinsell. Methuen, 1958.

Wessex before the Celts. J. F. S. Stone. Thames and Hudson, 1958.

Wessex from the Air. O. G. S. Crawford and A. Keiller. Clarendon Press, 1928.

Field Archaeology as illustrated by Hampshire. J. P. Williams-Freeman. Macmillan and Co., Ltd., 1915.

Towns of Roman Britain. John Wacher. Batsford, 1972.

Roman Silchester. G. C. Boon. Parrish, 1957.

Town and County in Roman Britain. A. L. F. Rivet. Hutchinson, 1958.

Excavations at Clausentum, 1951-4. M. Alwyn Cotton and P. W. Gathercole. H. M. Stationery Office, 1958.

Saxon Architecture in Hampshire. A. R. and P. M. Green. Warren and Son, 1951.

The Anglo-Saxon Chronicle, ed. D. Whitelock, D. Douglas, and S. Tucker. Eyre and Spottiswood, 1961.

The Winchester Psalter. Francis Wormald. Harvey Miller and Medcalf, 1973.

The Benedictional of St. Ethelwold. Francis Wormald. Faber and Faber, 1960.

Saxon Southampton. Southampton Archaeological Research Committee, 1975.

Two Anglo-Saxon Cemeteries at Winnall. A. L. Meaney and Sonia Chadwick Hawkes. Society for Medieval Archaeology, 1970.

The Coming of Christianity to Anglo-Saxon England. Henry Mayr-Harting. Batsford, 1972.

Winchester Excavations, 1949-60, Vol. I. Barry Cunliffe. City of Winchester Museums and Libraries Committee, 1964-7.

Anglo-Saxon Charters, ed. P. H. Sawyer. Royal Historical Society, 1968.

The Small Towns of Hampshire; the Archaeological and Historical Implications. Michael Hughes. Hampshire Archaeological Committee, 1976.

Excavations near Winchester Cathedral. M. Biddle. Wykeham Press, 1964.

Open Spaces in Hampshire. Barbara Carpenter Turner (3rd edition, 1970). Hampshire County Council.

Winchester. The Development of an Early Capital. Martin Biddle, 1973.

The Domesday Geography of South-east England, ed. H. C. Darby and E. M. J. Campbell. C.U.P., 1962.

'William the Conqueror's March through Hampshire in 1066'. F. B. Baring. H.F.C. *Proceedings,* VIII, Pt. II, 1915.

The Plans and Topography of Medieval Towns in England and Wales. C.B.A. Research Report No. 14, 1976.

The Ancient Usages of the City of Winchester. J. S. Furley. Oxford, 1927.

Building in England down to 1540. L. F. Salzman. Clarendon Press, 1952.

Italian Merchants and Shipping in Southampton, 1270-1600. A. A. Ruddock. Southampton Record Society, 1951.

'Four centuries of farming systems in Hampshire'. G. E. Fussell. H.F.C. *Proceedings,* XVIII, Pt. 3.

Compton. J. S. Drew. Warren and Son, 1959.

The Economic and Social History of an English Village (Crawley). W. C. B. and E. C. Gras. Harvard, 1930.

Pipe Roll of the Bishopric of Winchester, 1210-1211. N. R. Holt. University of Manchester Press, 1964.

Winchester Yields: A Study in Medieval Agricultural Productivity. J. Z. Titow. Cambridge University Press, 1972.

History of the King's Works. Vols. I and II. The Middle Ages (H.M.S.O., 1963). R. Allen Brown, H. M. Colvin, and J. S. Taylor.

Merdone. D. L. Peach and M. Meek. I.B.M., 1972.

The Beaulieu Cartulary, ed. by S. F. Hockey. Southampton Record Series Publications, 1975.

The Cartulary of God's House, Southampton. Vols. I and II, ed. by J. M. Kaye. Southampton Record Series Publications, 1976.

The Lands of Quarr Abbey. S. F. Hockey. University of Leicester Press, 1970.

Register of John de Pontissara, ed. C. Deedes. Canterbury and York Society, 1915.

Register of Henry Woodlock, ed. A. W. Goodman. Canterbury and York Society, 1940.

Register of William of Wykeham, ed. T. F. Kirby. Hampshire Record Society, 1894.

'The Stockbridge Elections'. Rosalind Hill. H.F.C. *Proceedings,* XXIII, Pt. III, 1968.

In a Liberal Tradition. V. Bonham-Carter. Constable, 1960.

General View of the Agriculture of Hampshire and the Isle of Wight. Charles Vancouver, 1813.

The South Western Railway. Hamilton Ellis. Allen and Unwin, 1950.

Canals of Southern England. Charles Hadfield. Phoenix House, 1955.

English Prison Hulks. W. Branch-Johnson. Johnson, 1957.

The Military Memorials of Winchester Cathedral. R. F. K. Goldsmith. Friends of the Cathedral, 1974.

The Royal Hampshire Regiment. Alan Wykes. Hamish Hamilton, 1968.

Hampshire: Industrial Archaeology: a Guide, ed. Monica Ellis. Southampton University Industrial Archaeology Group, 1975.

A Gazeteer of Hampshire Breweries. M. F. Tingle. Southampton University Industrial Archaeology Group.

A Gazeteer of Brick and Tile Works in Hampshire. W. C. F. White. Southampton University Industrial Archaeology Group.

Buriton and its People. E. M. Yates. Petersfield Papers, No. 22, 1976.

The Black Death on the Estates of the See of Winchester. A. E. Levett. Oxford Studies in Social and Legal History, I. Oxford University Press, 1916.

The Black Death. P. Ziegler. History Book Club, 1969.

The Churches of Medieval Winchester. Barbara Carpenter Turner. Warren and Son, 1957.

Winchester Cathedral Cartulary, ed. A. F. Goodman. Warren and Son, 1927.

A History of Winchester College. A. F. Leach, Duckworth, 1899.

History of The Vyne. Charles C. Chute. Jacob and Johnson, Winchester, 1888.

Parish Registers of the Archdeaconry of Winchester. W. F. Fearon and J. F. Williams. Warren and Son.

'Hampshire Recusants at the time of Elizabeth I'. J. E. Paul. H.F.C. *Proceedings,* XXII, Pt. II, 1959.

Registers of Bishop Gardiner, Poynet and White. Various editors. Canterbury and York Society, 1930.

History of the Andover Grammar School. A C. Bennett, E. Parsons. Parsons, Andover, 1930.

The Civil War in Hampshire. G. N. Godwin. Gilbert, Southampton, 1904.

Dean Young's Diary, ed. F. Goodman. S.P.C.K., 1923.

Quarter Sessions Government in Hampshire in the Seventeenth Century, ed. J. S. Furley. Warren and Son, n.d.

Poor Law in Hampshire throughout the Centuries. Hampshire Archivists Group, Publication No. 1, 1970.

The Scandal of the Andover Workhouse. Ian Anstruther. Geoffrey Bles, 1973.

Four centuries of Farming Systems in Hampshire, 1500-1900. G. E. Fussell. H.F.C. *Proceedings,* XVIII, Pt. 3, 1952.

The Story of Bournemouth. David S. Young. Robert Hale, 1957.

The Story of Aldershot. Howard N. Cole. Gale and Polden, 1951.

Southampton. A. Temple Patterson. Macmillan, 1970.

Enter Rumour, R. B. Martin. Faber and Faber, 1962.

Hampshire and the Isle of Wight (The Buildings of England Series). Nikolaus Pevsner and David Lloyd. Penguin, 1967.

Guides and Brief Histories of the new District Council areas (published by the local authority concerned):

    Hart.

    Basingstoke.

    New Forest.

    Test Valley.

    Winchester.

The Hampshire County Handbook and Industrial Survey (Hampshire on the eve of Reorganisation), n.d. Paul Cave Publications.

Hampshire Reorganised. First Annual report, 1975 (H.C.C.).

Ordained in Powder. R. P. Butterfield. Herald Press, Farnham, 1966.

Whigs and Hunters. E. P. Thompson. Allen Lane, 1975.

Historical Miscellany of Basingstoke. G. Willis *et aliis.* Crosby Press, 1972.

'Field Systems and Enclosures in Hampshire'. W. E. Tate. H.F.C. *Proceedings*, Vol. XVI, Pt. 3. 1947.

Edward the Confessor. Frank Barlow. Eyre and Spottiswoode, 1970.

Medieval Southampton. Colin Platt. Routledge & Kegan Paul, 1973.

Index

Abbotstone 82, 84
Abbotts Ann 19, 57
Ace, Benedict 43
Adams family 97
Aelfric, ealdorman 27, 29
agriculture 13, 14, 15, 16, 19, 24, 35, 49-53, 58, 60, 70, 81, 82, 86, 97, 99, 100
Aldershot 97, 99, 100, 118
Alfred, K. 26, 27, 29, 30, 31
Alresford 46, 87, 90, 92, 119
Alton 34, 36, 39, 81, 84, 90, 97, 99, 116; Eggars Grammar School, 91
Amport 57
Andover 19, 71, 90, 115, 119, 120; growth of 100-1, 109; medieval 42, 44, 45; Saxon 30, 34; schools at 75, 91
Andrew(e)s, Lancelot, Bp. of Winchester 76; Richard 98
Anstey 34
architecture 54, 87, 99; domestic 39, 47, 50, 54, 70-1, 73-4, 87; ecclesiastical 54, 62, 99
Aslett family 83
Atrebates 15, 17
Austen, Jane 82, 92
Avington Park 84, 87
Avon, R. 15

Baigent, F. J. 95
Barton Stacey 102, 107
Basing 39, 70; House 76, 78, 118
Basingstoke 34, 92, 97, 100, 109, 113, 115, 116, 120; medieval 39, 46, 57
Bassett, Thomas, Dr. 74
Beacon Hill 50
Beaulieu 13; Abbey 54, 60, 68
Belgae 16, 17
Bere Mill 97
Bethell family 74
Binstead, I. of Wight 50
Birinus, St. 25, 26
Bishop's Meon 103
Bishop's Waltham 14, 87, 91, 119; bps' palace at 50, 61, 64
Bishopstoke 108, 109
Bitterne (Clausentum) 17, 19, 21, 64
Black Death 48, 50, 55, 57-8, 59, 65, 104
Blois, Henry de, Bp. of Winchester 36, 39, 40, 61-2
Boarhunt 35
Boscombe Down East 14
Botley 86, 97, 107, 119
Bournemouth 92, 96, 97, 108, 109, 117; as seaside resort 98-9, 100
Brading, I. of Wight 19, 57
Bramdean 105
Bramshill 70
Breamore Priory 60, 69
Broadlands 78
Brockenhurst 69

Broughton 92
Bucklers Hard 97, 118
Burghclere 14, 50, 55
Buriton 71
Bursledon 98
Bury Hill 15
Butser Hill 14, 118

Candover 38
Capell, Arthur 78
Capon, William, Rev. 75, 91
Carisbrooke, I. of Wight 21, 117; Castle 78, 105
Carter family 84-5; John 84
Catuvellauni 15
Cenwealh, K. 25, 26
Chamberlayne, Thomas 108
Champfleur, John 91
Channel Islands 63, 96
Charles, K., I, 76, 78; II, 79
Chawton 34, 38, 117
Cheriton, battle of 78
Chessel Down, I. of Wight 24
Chilbolton Down 13
Chilcomb 49; Priory 35
Christchurch 14, 26, 35, 82, 98, 99, 109, 115, 116; Castle 36; Priory 57, 60
Christian church 71, 80, 87, 88, 90, 96-7; estates of 34-5, 39; medieval 36, 57, 59, 64, 65; and Reformation 66, 69, 104; Roman 21-2; Saxon 25-6, 29, 30-1, 102; see also Winchester, Diocese of; monasteries
Chute, Challoner 79
Clarke, Alured, Rev. 87
Clere 35, 64
Cliddesden 92
Cobbett, William 49, 86, 107
Colbury 70
Collier (Collyer) family 83, 84
Colson, John 93
Colt, Anne, Abbess of Romsey 68
Compton 52, 57, 71, 87, 90, 105
Corhampton 35
Cotton family 71; Reynell 91
Cowdreye, Alice, Abbess of Romsey 68
Craan, Hugh de 47
Crawley 52
Cromwell, Oliver 78
Crondall 53, 57, 84; manor of 49, 104
Crux Easton 81
Cynegils, K. 25

Damerham 19
Danebury 13, 15, 118
Daniel, bp. of Winchester 23, 31
Dawtrey, Sir John 74
Defoe, Daniel 81, 86, 98
Delmé, Peter 85
Dickens, Charles 99
Domesday Book 32-4, 35, 37, 38, 53, 103, 114

126